*A LifeBuilder*

CU00866770

The STORY *of* GOD *and* MAN

The Unfolding Drama of the Bible

12 studies
for individuals or groups

Robbie F. Castleman

with notes for leaders

*For my students – may you be an answer to the prayer of Jesus as you are
sanctified by the truth of God's Word (John 17:17)*

☞ Scripture Union is an international Christian charity working with
churches in more than 130 countries providing resources to bring the good
news about Jesus Christ to children, young people and families – and to
encourage them to develop spiritually through the Bible and prayer. As well
as a network of volunteers, staff and associates who run holidays, church-
based events and school Christian groups, Scripture Union produces a wide
range of publications and supports those who use their resources through
training programmes.

Scripture Union, 207-209 Queensway, Bletchley, MK2 2EB, UK.
e-mail: info@scriptureunion.org.uk
website: www.scriptureunion.org.uk

Scripture Union Australia: Locked Bag 2, Central Coast Business Centre,
NSW 2252 – www.su.org.au

ISBN 978 1 84427 382 9

First published as *The Story of Scripture* in the United States by InterVarsity
Press 2008. Published in Great Britain by Scripture Union 2008.

British Library Cataloguing-in-Publication data: a catalogue record for this
book is available from the British Library.

Printed in Singapore by Tien Wah Press.

Contents

Getting the Most Out of
The Story of God and Man

In a fast-paced culture of information overload many people master the art of living by sound bites and quick decisions. The practice of abbreviation used in text messaging, e-mail, two-minute news summaries, instant messaging and blog sites, combined with increasingly short attention spans, it's easy to know a little bit of many things, but never the depth of a few things. When it comes to the knowledge of the Bible, many people know bits and pieces, favorite stories and characters, but they don't know the story that is really *one* story in Scripture.

Many people have started (many times!) "to read through the whole Bible," but they give up right around Leviticus. Some people assume that the Bible is like a two-thousand-piece puzzle—best left to those who like working on puzzles and get paid for it. Others dismiss the Bible as an irrelevant story about some very messy, violent and incredibly naive people. And lots of disciples of Jesus, who want to mature and progress in their understanding of their faith, desire to understand the story of God's people in a comprehensive and helpful way. This LifeBuilder is written for all of the above.

The Bible is composed of sixty-six books written over a period of at least 1,350 years—originally written, for the most part, in two languages by people who encountered God and through whom God tells the story of his faithfulness to really awful but beloved people. It's a great story. For Christians, it's a story we need to know well so that we can tell it better.

To study the story of Scripture from Genesis to Revelation in twelve studies is an adventure that will simply make you want to take the trip again. This guide is not designed as an exhaustive exploration of all the Bible contains. That takes a lifetime of studying and savoring the Word of God, no matter how much or how little you know. This LifeBuilder will help you put the story of God and his people together so that you'll know how all the parts and people fit, and the stories within the story will make more sense.

This study should help you gain your bearings, to know where you are headed in the life of faith, to misunderstand directions less often, and to understand why you're on this journey of faith in the first place.

There are several features of this study guide that are necessary in order to cover so much territory in so little time. First, there are comments along the way to summarize important history that happens between passages, as well as to help relate major themes that mark the overall story of Scripture. Second, at the end of each study, there are suggestions for "Now or Later" to help you continue to study the story, and there are also suggestions for reading "Between the Times" to provide guidance in reading what happens between the scenes. Third, the Leader's Notes are quite extensive and often include background notes, suggestions for other Bible passages that build on or underscore the idea being discussed, or they point to the ultimate meaning or fulfillment of the whole story. I think it would be helpful for everyone who uses this guide to refer to the Leader's Notes throughout the study. Finally, in the back of the guide, I've included a basic timeline that will help you see the sequence of biblical events and characters—as well as when each individual "story within the story" takes place historically.

Too often, people read the Bible just looking for sound bites to put on plaques and pillows, calendars and car bumpers. But Scripture is not a series of clichés meant to make us feel better. If we don't know the whole story, it's easy to treat Scripture like a sanctified horoscope. Also, Scripture is not simply a deposit of true propositional statements that can be pulled apart from their stories. Knowing the whole story of Scripture is vital if we are to learn the truth in Scripture. It is my hope that *The Story of God and Man* will help you read the Bible for the rest of your life, and like a child with a favorite book we will say to our Father, "Oh, read it one more time!"

Suggestions for Individual Study

1. As you begin each study, pray that God will speak to you through his Word.

2. Read the introduction to the study and respond to the personal reflection question or exercise. This is designed to help you focus on God and on the theme of the study.

3. Each study deals with a particular passage so that you can delve into the author's meaning in that context. Read and reread the passage to be studied. The questions are written using the language of the New International Version, so you may wish to use that version of the Bible. The New Revised Standard Version is also recommended.

4. This is an inductive Bible study, designed to help you discover for yourself what Scripture is saying. The study includes three types of questions. *Observation* questions ask about the basic facts: who, what, when, where and how. *Interpretation* questions delve into the meaning of the passage. *Application* questions help you discover the implications of the text for growing in Christ. These three keys unlock the treasures of Scripture.

Write your answers to the questions in the spaces provided or in a personal journal. Writing can bring clarity and deeper understanding of yourself and of God's Word.

5. It might be good to have a Bible dictionary handy. Use it to look up any unfamiliar words, names or places.

6. Use the prayer suggestion to guide you in thanking God for what you have learned and to pray about the applications that have come to mind.

7. You may want to go on to the suggestion under "Now or Later," or you may want to use that idea for your next study.

Suggestions for Members of a Group Study

1. Come to the study prepared. Follow the suggestions for individual study mentioned above. You will find that careful preparation will greatly enrich your time spent in group discussion.

2. Be willing to participate in the discussion. The leader of your group will not be lecturing. Instead, he or she will be encouraging the members of the group to discuss what they have learned. The leader will be asking the questions that are found in this guide.

3. Stick to the topic being discussed. Your answers should be based on the verses which are the focus of the discussion and not on outside authorities such as commentaries or speakers. These studies focus on a particular passage of Scripture. Only rarely should you refer to other portions of the Bible. This allows for everyone to participate in in-depth study on equal ground.

4. Be sensitive to the other members of the group. Listen attentively when they describe what they have learned. You may be surprised by their insights! Each question assumes a variety of answers. Many questions do not have "right" answers, particularly questions that aim at meaning or application. Instead the questions push us to explore the passage more thoroughly.

When possible, link what you say to the comments of others. Also, be affirming whenever you can. This will encourage some of the more hesitant members of the group to participate.

5. Be careful not to dominate the discussion. We are sometimes so eager to express our thoughts that we leave too little opportunity for others to respond. By all means participate! But allow others to also.

6. Expect God to teach you through the passage being discussed and through the other members of the group. Pray that you will have an enjoyable and profitable time together, but also that as a result of the study you will find ways that you can take action individually and/or as a group.

7. Remember that anything said in the group is considered confidential and should not be discussed outside the group unless specific permission is given to do so.

8. If you are the group leader, you will find additional suggestions at the back of the guide.

1

The Beginning of the Story

Characters, Setting, Plot

Genesis 1—2

The opening scenes of the story are intended to introduce us to who God is through what God did in creating the heavens and the earth. And they are intended to show God's particular love for human beings and God's intention for our relationships in caring for what God created and for each other.

GROUP DISCUSSION. On a piece of paper, write down your main impression of the first two chapters of Genesis. Have someone collect the papers and sort them into piles of summary answers. Briefly discuss the results for the group and end by praying for helpful insight into what God would have the group learn from the beginning of God's story in Genesis.

PERSONAL REFLECTION. Recall discussions or thoughts you may have had about the creation accounts in the first and second chapters of Genesis. What do you consider important or unimportant about these ideas? Ask God to help you set aside those ideas for a time in order to see these texts in a fresh and insightful way.

The first two chapters of the Bible are the foundation for the rest of the Old and New Testaments. In this study we will see how God's acts of creation reflect his character and purposes for the cosmos, all that is contained within time and space. *Read Genesis 1—2:3.*

1. List a summary of the sequence of creative acts. Use the words following "God said, 'Let'" as a basic outline.

2. Beside the verb *said*, what other action verbs are used throughout this passage to indicate the different ways God created?

3. Note the final refrain in each section of verses: "And there was evening, and there was morning." What does this suggest to you about the nature of God's work?

The seventh day ends differently. What do we learn from that?

4. Reflect on God's declaration of creation as "good" (v. 31). How can this influence your attitude concerning creation care and bodily existence?

5. What distinguishes the account of God's creation of human beings (Genesis 1:26-30) as compared to the rest of creation?

6. No distinction should be made between *image* and *likeness*, as these words are used synonymously throughout the Old and New Testaments. How does an "image" of something help us understand what the "original" is like?

7. What aspects of God's character are reflected in *how* God chose to create?

8. How should women and men reflect similar characteristics in work and in relationships with one another?

During the cosmic creation account, the name *Elohim* is used to refer to our creator God who is *beyond* time and space. However, the second chapter of Genesis continues by relating the story as personal and particular, and God is now presented as the Lord God. *Yahweh* is used to refer to our God who is in personal relationship with his people *within* time and space (see Exodus 3:15). *Yahweh* is revealed as the same creator God of the cosmos, and in the second chapter of Genesis, the creation account narrows to describe God's intimate and personal relationship with a man and woman to whom he will reveal himself more fully. *Read Genesis 2:15-25.*

9. Along with the generous provisions the Lord God makes for the man, there is also a prohibition that demands faith and obedience from the man. How is the idea of human freedom and free will in relationship to God's sovereign rule reflected in this part of the story (vv. 15-17)?

10. In the personal and relational account of humanity's creation, the Lord God declares for the first time that something is "not good." Identify what is "not good" and summarize what God does to make it right (Genesis 2:18, 20-23).

11. When the man first sees the woman, what does he celebrate about her?

12. How might this account of the first human couple counteract the common idea of "the opposite sex," an idea which highlights the differences between men and women?

13. How have the Genesis accounts of how things were supposed to be enriched your understanding of God's hopes for creation and the human family?

14. In what specific ways could your relationship with others, both at work and in the home, better reflect the image of God?

Spend time thanking God for the goodness of creation, both for its provisions and for other people. Pray for God's wisdom in knowing how to be a good steward of creation and a godly person in family relationships.

Now or Later

In light of what you learned in looking carefully at the first two chapters of Genesis, write a paragraph reflecting on how the beginning of the story influences your understanding of the rest of the story as you know it. Include your present ideas and thoughts as well as questions that you want to continue to explore as the story of Scripture unfolds.

Between the Times: No one knows how long Eden flourished as a place of harmony, rest and goodness, but the creation story resumes in Genesis 3 with the introduction of a beguiling intruder.

2

The Story Continues

A Twist in the Storyline

Genesis 3

Most people can recall a time during childhood when they began to recognize that something was not right deep inside their lives. I remember the time my five-year-old son burst into tears during the prayer of confession time in worship. He was full of remorse and tearfully repented from cheating his little brother out of half a chocolate donut. In the light of a liturgical moment, a childhood conviction was used by God to help my son begin to understand what it means to be a sinner.

GROUP DISCUSSION. Write a short confession of a sinful childhood act on a piece of paper and put in a basket. If you feel comfortable, have a drawing and try to guess who's who!

PERSONAL REFLECTION. Recall a time from your childhood (or later life) when you began to recognize that something was deeply flawed in your being and character. Pray about sinful habits that still mark your life and give thanks for God's promise to never give up on you and that all things will be made right once again.

No one knows how long the man *(ish)* and the woman *(ishshah)* lived, worked and enjoyed God's bountiful provisions in the paradise of Eden. Genesis 5:3 tells us that the man, now designated as Adam, was 130 years old when his third son, Seth, was born. Seth's birth followed the murder of Adam's son, Abel, by his brother, Cain (Genesis 4:1-10). What happened in the 130 years between the joy and unashamed gladness of chapter 2 and the competitive hatred and fratricide that breaks God's heart and fractures the first family in chapter 4? For this story of disobedience, rebellion, loss and consequence—and the beginning of God's plan to make things right again—we turn to Genesis 3. *Read Genesis 3.*

---

1. Note how the tempter casts doubt on God's words. How is doubt introduced and how does this contradict what God has said in the previous chapter (vv. 1-5)?

---

2. Verse 6 is considered the first outline of the "anatomy of sin" in the Scripture. Summarize this progressive descent into disobedience in your own words.

---

3. When have you noted this "anatomy of sin" in your own life or in the life of celebrities or public figures? Within appropriate boundaries, summarize some clear examples.

---

4. Verses 7-13 recount the immediate aftermath of the man and woman's disobedience to the command of the Lord God. Study the scene, its characters and what happens. Note who it is that initiates the confrontation and how God prompts the confession of sin from each person. What do you think is significant about this?

5. Note how the human couple attempts to place the blame on another in this passage. Who or what do we attempt to blame for our sinful behavior?

6. Verses 14-19 record the judgment of God concerning the tempter-serpent, the woman and the man. What do you find to be significant in the fact that the Lord God only used the word *curse* in his address to the tempter-serpent and in his statement of what would happen to the earth? How have you seen the consequences of the man's and woman's action in your own life?

7. The cursing of the tempter-serpent (v. 15) in relationship to the woman also involves the generations of children that will be born from her. The promise of one human child to be born who will "crush" the head of the serpent, a final and fatal defeat, is revealed in the New Testament in Jesus the Son of God. Suggest stories within Scripture that illustrate how the sin of woman and man in Eden is passed down to all people.

8. In verses 16-19 the consequences for the woman and man are outlined. What are they?

How are they still a part of our lives today?

---

9. In verse 20, the renaming of the woman *(ishshah)* by the man *(ish)* indicates a disruption of the perfect fitness of their relationship, even though the name given the woman, Eve, is both benevolent and hopeful. How does this part of the story help you identify continuing consequences of the Fall in relationships between men and women?

---

10. The chapter ends with the Lord God's reflection on what humankind's disobedience means: it leads to death (only the Creator, not creatures, can rightly handle the knowledge of good and evil!). Why do you think God guards the way to the tree of life now that Adam and Eve know good from evil?

11. Consider how the use of tools makes work less toilsome and how some medical discoveries alleviate pain. Think about how things you use (tools, pain relievers) in everyday life deal with the consequences of the Fall. What do those things indicate about the losses incurred in the Fall?

Take some time to silently reflect on this story of the Fall and pray to confess personal sin to God. Close your time by praying aloud words of thanksgiving for the story of Scripture, which culminates in the forgiveness of sin through the final sacrifice of Jesus Christ.

Now or Later

In light of Genesis 3:22-24, read Revelation 22:1-5 and discover how the tree of life is restored in the new heaven and new earth of God's eternal kingdom. Find a hymnal and sing the doxology as a song of praise for such a glorious ending to the story of Scripture.

Between the Times: Read Genesis 4—11.

3

The Story Is
Our Story

Everyone Has a Part

Genesis 12:1-5; 15

After the first family was banished from the Garden of Eden, Scripture records their descendants and highlights episodes of an emerging humanity that is full of longing, learning, turmoil and attempts at faithfulness. The first "worship war," murder and the beginning of prayer occur in chapter 4, the deepening of rebellion and sin and the grace of God manifest again through one family in chapter 5, God's rescue of creation through judgment and cleansing are shown in the story of Noah and the ark in chapters 6-9, the post-flood descendants are listed and the story of God scattering prideful people who wanted to make a name for themselves are told in chapters 10 and 11. All these stories portray patterns of human sinfulness and the persistence of God to redeem all that had been lost.

GROUP DISCUSSION: Make a list of the variety of ways God communicates with people. Discuss which have been most helpful when significant family decisions have to be made (like moving to a new place or changing jobs).

PERSONAL REFLECTION. Recall a time of change that required a step of faith when the outcome was not at all certain. What did you learn about yourself and about God's faithfulness through that experience?

In Abraham's part of the story, God continues his plan to create a family of faith through which he will bring forth a nation of people who will embody his story and herald his saving love for the whole creation. Abraham's story marks the first "dateable" event in Scripture, and most scholars date this story around 2000 B.C. *Read Genesis 12:1-5.*

1. If possible, look at a map in the back of a Bible or in a Bible atlas and see the route from Haran to Canaan. Middle Canaan was approximately 450 miles south-southwest of ancient Haran. What challenges might Abraham's caravan expect for such a journey in his day?

2. Read the blessing in verses 2-3. How would you feel or what would you think about on hearing this promise?

3. Abraham does bring along members of his household with him (vv. 4-5). This may have been due to the traditions of the culture. The New Testament records that Jesus asked several of his disciples to leave all behind and to come and follow him. How have you found "leaving all" a challenge in being obedient to the direction of the Lord?

Abraham journeys throughout Canaan for some time searching for a place to settle, but much of the land needed to support his flocks is occupied by others. God continues to promise that someday Abraham's offspring will occupy the land. From place to place, the patriarch builds an altar and worships the Lord. Abraham journeys to Egypt to escape a famine (chapter 12), but returns to Canaan, resumes his nomadic journey and continues to build altars from place to place and call on the Lord (chapter 13). At one point a territorial war breaks out between nine tribal kings and Lot is abducted. Abraham takes over 300 men to rescue Lot, and after this trial, the patriarch is met by an extraordinary priest (chapter 14) to whom Abraham reaffirms his faith in and commitment to one God, "the LORD, God Most High, Creator of heaven and earth" (v. 22). *Read Genesis 15.*

---

4. How does Abraham identify his greatest challenge in believing God's promise concerning the inheritance of Canaan?

---

5. How does Abraham's concern both hinder and help his faith at this time?

---

6. Note how Genesis 15:5 is a parallel to God's promise made in Genesis 13:16-18. How does the visual imagery God uses both challenge and encourage Abraham's faith?

7. Contrast Abraham's faith expressed in Genesis 15:6 and 15:8. What does it mean to believe *and* act on that belief as a dynamic of true faith?

8. Describe the scene that follows Abraham's question (vv. 9-17).

9. As the sun goes down (signaling a new day beginning in this Jewish story), the text indicates that this increasing darkness included more than just the night sky. How is Abraham described, and what does this indicate about his experience?

10. What details does God reveal to Abraham about his offspring in verses 13-16?

How might these details help Abraham's faith in God's promise to him?

11. The New Testament recounts the faith of Abraham displayed in this story as a way of encouraging God's people to trust God's plan of salvation by a radical investment of faith. How is your faith in God's plan of salvation, which is revealed throughout the story of Scripture, similar to that of Abraham's?

Spend time praising God for his faithfulness in keeping his promise of salvation through faith.

Now or Later

Identify an area in your life where faith is particularly difficult. What about this situation seems "impossible"? Consider what God has clearly promised in the Scripture (and what is not promised) that might address this difficulty and help your faith.

Between the Times: Finish reading Genesis.

4

The Story Continues

A World Premiere

Exodus 2:23—3:17

Being called on to reengage after a failed attempt is always a challenge. "I'll never do that again!" is a common declaration made after a fall from a horse or a disastrous result from an attempt to handle a problem. Getting "back in the saddle" takes courage even if you are confronted by the Word of God.

GROUP DISCUSSION. Recall times that you have heard God's challenging call to action. When have you been reluctant to accept?

PERSONAL REFLECTION. Recall a time in your life when you were reluctant to do something God clearly directed you to do. What made it hard to act? What did you learn from this time of challenging obedience?

Abraham and Sarah did have a child in their old age (Genesis 21:1-7). Isaac, the promised son and heir of the covenant, marries Rebecca and they have twin sons, Esau and Jacob (Genesis 24; 25:19-26). Jacob, whose name God changes to Israel (Genesis 32:22-28) builds the patriarchal family tree and family wealth by having many daughters and twelve sons, the second youngest being Joseph (Genesis 29—30:24).

Strife and jealousy, as well as an undaunting persistence to grow in faith and understanding, mark the intriguing saga of this family. Joseph is actually sold into Egyptian slavery by his elder brothers (Genesis 37:12-36), but Scripture makes it clear that despite sin God is at work to redeem and rescue this family that has grown from Abraham's faith (Genesis 45:7-8). Joseph's presence in Egypt is key to the family's survival during a severe famine, and the whole family journeys to Egypt and settles there long after the famine is over (Genesis 50:22-26). However, Egypt is not the land promised to Abraham and after several hundred years, the place of security becomes a place of slavery (Exodus 1:8-14). But God keeps his promise and raises up one who will deliver his people and lead them back to the land that God had promised to the offspring of Abraham. This deliverer was Moses.

The story continues as God confronts Moses and challenges his faith with a mission that, at first, Moses is reluctant to accept. *Read Exodus 2:23—3:17.*

---

1. Outline the variety of ways that the text makes it clear that God is fully aware of the plight of his people and has a plan for them.

---

2. In Exodus 2:23 God's people "cry out" and groan to him because of their circumstances. How is God's grace reflected in his response to the plight of his people (2:24-25)?

---

3. When have you complained, groaned, cried for help and experienced a long wait for God to act on your behalf?

How was this time of discontent and waiting both difficult and faith-building?

4. What is important about the encounter with "the angel of the Lord" (3:1-6)?

5. The text notes twice that the bush was aflame and yet not burned up (3:2-3). What do you think this is meant to indicate about the presence of God in this encounter with Moses?

6. Although God initiated this encounter, Moses, the shepherd of Midian, is told how he must conduct himself in the presence of God (3:4-6). God both calls Moses and sets limits on his approach. Note the response of Moses to the bush (3:4) and to how God first identifies himself (3:6).

In the passage, how do both Moses and God present the reality that should still inform how we worship God today?

7. What is Moses' initial response to the plan God outlines in Exodus 3:7-11?

How would you feel about God's response in 3:12 if you were Moses?

8. Note the second concern Moses raises in 3:13. How does God's answer in 3:14-15 sum up both God's character and God's plan?

---

9. Exodus 3:16-17 summarizes both the first step and the final outcome of God's plan. Why would both be important to Moses at this time?

---

10. God's name indicates God's character. If you had a name that represented your character, what would your name be today?

What name would you like to grow into as one of God's people? And what changes or additions to your life would help you get there?

Spend time praising God for his perfect holiness, sovereign plan and transforming power.

Now or Later

Spend some time in thoughtful prayer about the names of those closest to you. What transforming "name" would you like to see them grow into? Thank God, who keeps his promise to help us become who we truly are in Christ Jesus (Philippians 1:6).

Between the Times: Read Exodus 1—20 and 31—34:10; Joshua 1; Judges 2:6-23; and Ruth 4:13-22.

5

Knowing the Story

Studying the Script

2 Samuel 6

In the pages of Scripture we see God call forth a variety of leaders.

God keeps his promise to his people and delivers them, under the leadership of Moses, from the bondage of Egypt. On Mount Sinai God gives Moses his Law with detailed instructions for worship and how God's people are to live. The law is written, recorded and copied after that, even being summarized and rewritten as the book of Deuteronomy (Deuteronomy means "second law").

After Moses dies, Joshua leads God's people back into Canaan and reestablishes the people of Israel in their Promised Land. When Joshua dies, leadership is provided by judges. However, the book of Judges makes it clear that God's people struggle greatly to sustain faithfulness to Yahweh and a holy separation from the surrounding idolatrous nations. In cycle after cycle of sinfulness, suffering, repentance and finally deliverance, the book of Judges ends by noting, "In those days Israel had no king; everyone did as he saw fit" (Judges 21:25).

The comforting and hopeful book of Ruth follows the book of Judges providing an intimate glimpse at one brave woman who did remember the story, knew God's Word and worked hard to be faithful to Yahweh in uncertain times.

As the period of the judges comes to a close, the people increasingly clamor for a king. David, who is the great-grandson of the faithful family in the book of Ruth, is the second king of Israel. In stark contrast to the unfocused and weak of reign of Saul, the first king (1 Samuel 8—31), David is a natural leader, gifted militarily, politically and spiritually. Militarily, David enlarges the borders of Israel and subdues many of her enemies. David unifies the tribes politically by establishing a new capital city through the conquest of Jerusalem—a city that previously belonged to no single tribe (2 Samuel 5). And, spiritually, David begins to unify Israel by centralizing the place of sacrificial worship in the capital city of Jerusalem.

GROUP DISCUSSION. What do you consider the most important marks of spiritual leaders? Have each person in the group offer one suggestion and list them on a large sheet of paper. At the end of the study, check off and add those that you see in this story of David.

PERSONAL REFLECTION. Think about a person whose leadership has personally influenced your life, for good or ill. What was helpful (or unhelpful at times) about the leadership of this person?

David's first step in the unification of Israel's worship is to bring the Ark of the Covenant into Jerusalem. The Ark of the Covenant was first crafted by the exiles from Egypt during the time of Moses. When Samuel, the last of the judges, was just a boy, the Ark had been unwisely taken into a battle with the Philistines and had subsequently been left in a small town near the border of Philistia (1 Samuel 4—7:1) for nearly seventy-five years. *Read 2 Samuel 6.*

1. In 2 Samuel 6:1-5, note the number of people David takes with him to bring the Ark to Jerusalem and the activities surrounding the occasion. What might be some of the reasons for the unfettered festive mood of David and the people (consider 2 Samuel 5:17-25 in your discussion)?

2. It is important to note that the Ark is being brought to Jerusalem in the same manner as the Philistines returned the Ark to Israel (1 Samuel 6:8), not according to the instructions for its transport by the Levites given in the law (Numbers 4:5-6; 15). Summarize the surprising end of the celebration described in 2 Samuel 6:6-11.

3. Why is David angry about the death of Uzzah?

4. What are some (implicit or explicit) dos and don'ts of corporate worship in the practices of your church?

How are these practices reflective of the development of worship in Scripture, the early church, national or ethnic culture, congregational tradition and identity with or independence from a denomination?

5. Note how long the Ark was in the care of Obed-Edom (v. 11) and contrast the changes made in the transportation of the Ark and the celebration of worship in verses 12-15. What are the differences in transport, music and overall mood between the first and second events?

6. Reread verse 9. How does the proper fear of the Lord relate to the contrasts noted in question 5?

7. Verses 17-19 summarize the festivities in Jerusalem as the Ark was brought into the city. How do these things indicate what David learned by going back and studying the Scripture concerning the Ark and the worship of Yahweh?

List the variety of activities that take place and suggest ways these things are reflected in how you worship with God's people today.

8. David's wife, Michal, is a daughter of Saul, Israel's first king. What are her concerns regarding the festivities (vv. 16, 20)? Consider David's initial response to Michal in verse 21 as you think of a variety of reasons for her attitude.

9. How are David's focus for worship (v. 21) and his understanding of humility before God important aspects of worship that please the Lord (v. 22)?

10. Check the list made from your group discussion at the beginning of the study (or recall the leader from your personal reflection). What characteristics of spiritual leadership have you noted in this study of David?

From these strengths and weaknesses, how can you mature as a spiritual leader and one who worships rightly?

---

11. What steps can you, your family and your congregation take to bolster a proper sense of care and reverence in corporate worship?

After a time of prayer focused on the adoration of the Lord, sing the doxology or another favorite and well-known hymn or song of praise to God.

Now or Later

Consider what you can do between now and the next time you attend corporate worship to be better prepared and more thoughtful as a worshiper.

Between the Times: Read 2 Samuel 7—1 Kings 3; 1 Kings 11:41—12:31.

6

Knowing the Story

A Remedy for Stage Fright

Isaiah 7:1-14

It's hard to have hope when you are completely surrounded by problems and outnumbered by people or situations. It's especially hard to trust God in a situation when people in power over you can't be trusted. When overwhelmed by enemies who are threatening your life, wouldn't it be astounding to be offered a sign from God, accompanied by a guarantee of deliverance or healing or hope—and not just for an ultimate "someday," but for the reality of the immediate situation! How hard would it be, however, in the face of overwhelming odds to really believe the person who delivered the message of such hard-to-believe hope?

GROUP DISCUSSION. Think about the worst childhood experience or adult crisis you have ever had. How did you react to well-meaning words of hope from others during those times? What helped or hindered your ability to "hear God" during those times?

PERSONAL REFLECTION. Family disloyalties or significant health threats are often the most complicated and painful situations in life. It is often helpful to have another person to aid in finding a solution that can lead to family reconciliation or the courage to face life-threatening illness. When it was difficult to trust God in the face of overwhelming odds, who has helped during times of strife in your life?

After the reign of Solomon, it is important to note the distinction between the two kingdoms: northern Israel/Ephraim and southern Judah. Israel/Ephraim, however, is continually corrupt and compromises the worship of Yahweh with a mixture of idolatry and increasing immorality. This Northern Kingdom never has a ruler who is faithful to the Lord. Judah has a history that includes both faithful and faithless kings. During times of revival and obedience, the worship of Yahweh flourishes, and Jerusalem is still their capital city and the unifying center of worship. The nation of Judah outlasts their northern cousins before being conquered by foreign enemies. The two kingdoms of Israel and Judah were sometimes allies against a common enemy, but sometimes one would make an alliance with a foreign nation against their kinsmen. This is the situation of our present study. Israel's alliance with a powerful foreign king threatens Judah, and the southern nation of Judah is vulnerable and Judah's king is very afraid. Into this threatening situation, God sends a prophet with a word of hope, assurance, guidance, judgment and promise.

In the story of Scripture, as seen in this study, God's greatest promises are often given to the weakest of God's people, to those who struggle to believe or even refuse to believe. *Read Isaiah 7:1-14.*

---

1. Identify the enemies of Judah and her king in verse 1, and discuss the terrifying dynamics of this threatening situation.

---

2. Reread verse two. How would it have felt to be in this situation?

3. This is the only instance in the Old Testament where a king of Judah is personified as "the house of David." What is this wording meant to communicate about God's perspective concerning this threatening situation?

4. Shear-Jashub, the name of Isaiah's son, means "a remnant shall return" and reflects God's promise not to forsake his people. Isaiah is sent with his son to the "aqueduct of the Upper Pool," because the Lord knew Ahaz would be there to check Jerusalem's water supply, which they would need for the expected siege against the city. Why are both the presence of Isaiah's son and the place of confrontation significant?

5. If you have ever felt as vulnerable and out of options as does Ahaz, what did you do or think about doing to protect or defend yourself?

6. Verse 4 contains God's imperatives for how Ahaz is to act and God's assessment of the enemies that are threatening Judah. How do both of these ideas reinforce each other?

7. Verses 5-9 are a prophecy about the demise of both Aram and Israel. If you were in Ahaz's situation, what would make this word from the Lord through his prophet hard to believe?

8. The last sentence in verse 9 is God's challenge to Ahaz and Judah, echoing the prophecy in verse 7. Essentially the king and the nation are being challenged to do nothing! When have you been challenged in such an absolute way to trust God to act on your behalf and to do nothing on your own behalf?

---

9. Verse 11 is one of the most amazing offers God ever makes an individual in Scripture. If God were to make you that offer today, how would you respond?

---

10. Why do you think Ahaz responds the way he does (v. 12)?

---

11. Note how Isaiah addresses Ahaz in verse 13. How does this suggest what is really at stake at this time of Judah's history?

---

12. God offers a surprising sign in verse 14. How does the historical context of this study deepen your understanding of this verse, which is so commonly associated (often out of context) with Christmas?

13. How can God's promise of eternal life and ultimate healing through the death and resurrection of Jesus help you have faith during some of life's most threatening times?

Consider an "impossibility" in your life. Pray for the faith to believe and trust the Lord with this situation or need that seems impossible.

Now or Later

Read Luke 1:26-38 and consider how the incarnation of God in Jesus is the ultimate sign that should help us in all "impossible" situations to be people who believe that God will keep his promises.

Between the Times: Read 2 Kings 17; 22—25:21.

7

The Story Continues

Taking It on the Road

Daniel 1

God's word through Isaiah to Ahaz proved true in every detail. The enemies of Judah, both Aram and the Northern Kingdom of Israel, are conquered by the Assyrians within sixty-five years of Isaiah's meeting with Ahaz at the aqueduct (Isaiah 7:1-14). However, as much as Judah considers the conquest of Israel as the judgment of God for disobedience and faithlessness, like Ahaz, the nation as a whole does not learn their lesson in order to avoid the same judgment. Judah, despite a few kings who bring revival and reformation for a time, becomes increasingly disobedient, idolatrous, immoral and faithless. Their judgment comes when the Babylonians, who had conquered the entire Assyrian empire, destroy Jerusalem and conquer Judah in 586 B.C.

In all the lands captured by Babylon, the best and brightest young leaders of every nation are taken to Babylon to be educated and in-doctrinated in Babylonian language and the cultural customs of the new empire. The story of Scripture continues as the exiles from Judah have to figure out how to be faithful to Yahweh in a land far away and very different from their Jewish homeland.

GROUP DISCUSSION. On a piece of paper write one or two sentences about the most "fish out of water" experience you have ever had.

Indicate where you were (a foreign country? the first time at your in-laws? a dormitory your first year in college?). When did you feel awkward and out of place, or when did you do something the "locals" found pretty weird? Don't put your name on the paper, but have a drawing and try to guess who's who.

PERSONAL REFLECTION. Recall a time when you were in a situation that made you feel like a "fish out of water." Journal about what made the situation awkward, embarrassing or just interesting. What did you learn from the experience that has helped you in other situations?

One of the Jewish leaders taken to Babylon is a young man named Daniel. In this study we will see how God is not confined to a promised land but continues his story through his promised people. Daniel and his friends have to understand the distinction between being faithful and being effective by learning how to be both without compromising what matters while under the authority of others. *Read Daniel 1.*

---

1. Verses 1-2 summarize the conquest of Judah and the destruction of Jerusalem. What do these verses focus on to highlight the hopelessness and defilement experienced by Daniel and the exiles?

---

2. What are the characteristics of the captives who the king wants to indoctrinate in order to serve the Babylonian court and promote its interests (vv. 3-4)?

Note some of the ways the indoctrination of the captives is to be accomplished. Why do you think he chooses these methods (vv. 4-5)?

3. Daniel and his friends refuse to take the royal food and wine (v. 8). Why do you think the Jewish captives choose this particular thing to "draw the line"?

4. What other things could Daniel and his friends have resisted or refused, but apparently did not?

5. When have you had to make up your mind about an issue, knowing that it is based on a nonnegotiable principle of faith? How did your mental resolve help guide your behavior, as well as strengthen your faith commitment at the time?

6. Note how the text indicates the sovereignty of God, acting behind the scenes to make a way for Daniel and his friends to be faithful. What is the official's initial response to Daniel's request?

7. How does Daniel's plan address both his desire as well as the official's concern (vv. 11-13)?

8. What are the short- (vv. 14-17) and long-term (vv. 18-20) outcomes of Daniel's plan? Note what, if anything, you see God doing.

9. Verse 21 records that Daniel serves the Babylonian empire until it is conquered by Cyrus the Persian. This indicates that Daniel served the royal dynasties of Babylonian leaders and, in fact, lived his entire life in exile. Day by day, year by year, Daniel makes decisions about how to be faithful to Yahweh and a good servant in a foreign land, seeking its benefit and prosperity. How do you experience this dynamic in your life?

10. Historically God's people have related to the world and to culture in one of three ways: (1) assimilation by giving in to culture and relieving the pressure that faithfulness demands; (2) withdrawal into a sheltered enclave within the world to avoid the pressure as much as possible; or (3) confronting culture with the aim of transforming it by engaging with the world, the foreign place, responsibly and without compromising one's ultimate allegiance to God. How do you see these three approaches in Christian people and communities today?

Pray about how you and your faith community can mature as faithful witnesses in a world that is not our home. Pray that God would give you the resolve needed to take the next step.

Now or Later

Take time to read Daniel 3, and discuss how Daniel's three friends display their faith in a threatening situation.

Between the Times: Read Ezra 1; 4; Nehemiah 1; 2; 4—7:4; 8.

8

The Story Continues

After the Theater Burns Down

Haggai 1—2:19

People who have returned to houses and hometowns completely devastated by flood, fire or tornadoes (or war) can testify to the mental, emotional and spiritual exhaustion that makes doing anything harder and more costly, and the pace of recovery is often discouraging. It is often the next generation that reassesses and reenergizes the work that needs to be done. After Hurricane Katrina devastated the Gulf Coast, it was often the people who moved into the area—either as temporary volunteers or permanent residents—who helped those who suffered the most to see the possibilities of rebuilding and helped them muster up the energy to get the ball rolling.

GROUP DISCUSSION. In North America, "compassion fatigue" is a fairly common response after national or global disasters are reported (usually with heartbreaking pictures) week after week, month after month, year after year. The need for volunteers, funding, sponsorships, clothing drives and other donations sometimes get so overwhelming that we just stop looking and listening, at least for a time, to focus on our own lives and take a break. When have you experienced "compassion fatigue" and how did you handle it?

PERSONAL REFLECTION. Recall a time when you felt absolutely over-whelmed with "everything that needs to be done." What helped you cope? Who came along to spur you on and give you hope or help?

Just as the Babylonians overthrew the Assyrian Empire, the Persians now conquer the Babylonians. The Persians, however, want a richer and more stable empire. The Babylonian hope of a monoculture built on the forced indoctrination of young leaders left parts of the empire vulnerable and underdeveloped. The Persians reverse this policy and encourage the expatriot leadership to return to their homelands, re-build and populate their cities, and worship their own gods. The Old Testament books of Ezra and Nehemiah record the return of the Jew-ish exiles to Judah's territory and the reestablishment of a vassal state under Persian rule. After years of war and at least seventy years in exile, only a small percentage (scholars usually estimate 10 to 30 per-cent at the most) of Jewish exiles return to Judah. The challenge of re-building their culture, reestablishing their livelihoods and renewing religious practice is simply too much for most of them. Both Haggai and Zechariah were probably born in exile and returned as children with the faithful remnant of Judah around 537 B.C. Seventeen years later, around 520 B.C., Haggai received a word from the Lord and got the ball rolling! *Read Haggai 1:1-11.*

---

1. The record of Haggai's ministry in this book covers a period only four months long. How many times are phrases like "the word of the Lord" or "what the Lord Almighty says" used in the passage?

How are these expressions different from an optimistic and well-intended "pep talk"?

2. What problems are addressed by the Lord through the prophet (1:2-4, 6, 9)?

3. Note the admonitions repeated in 1:5 and 1:7. Self-assessment can be helpful in reordering priorities. When has reflecting on situations in your life (or your faith community) helped you (or your church) discern priorities and move ahead with what needs to be done?

4. What is the first step God directs the people to take (1:8)?

Notice the reason that is given in the text for this first step necessary to rebuild the temple. How does God's valuing the "means" as well as the "ends" encourage your first steps of faithfulness?

5. The consequence of long-term neglect and questionable priorities in rebuilding Jerusalem are indicated and explained in 1:10-11. How would this situation, which has compounded the recovery effort, also influence the ability of the people to be responsive to God's word at this time?

Read Haggai 1:12—2:9.

6. Note the length of time indicated by Haggai 1:1 and 1:15. What does this period communicate about the response of the governor, high priest and people of Judah?

How does the attitude of the people (1:12) relate to the activity they undertake?

7. What encouragement is offered to the people and what promises are made (2:3-9)?

Read Haggai 2:10-19.

8. It can be very difficult to appreciate progress in rebuilding a place or reinvesting in a person. It's even harder when you remember "how things used to be." Discuss similar experiences you've had and what helped you hope and keep working during those times.

9. Haggai presents two situations and asks for a ruling (2:12-13). What is asked and what answer is given?

10. God reminds the people that holiness, like true splendor, is his to give and theirs to protect and honor (2:14). Note the repetition of the statement in Haggai 1:5, 7 in Haggai 2:15. How does this "reality check" about how things used to be serve to keep the people focused on the present challenge?

What promise does God make on this important day?

11. God promises his blessing for this new temple, even though its glory will be different from the glitter of Solomon's masterpiece. In times of overwhelming challenge, how has remembrance, hard work and a commitment to holiness helped you come to a time of blessing and promise for the future?

Spend time worshiping God for his faithfulness and grace in times of rebuilding.

Now or Later

Finish reading Haggai to discover how the story is resolved.

Between the Times: Read Malachi 2—3:2 and the Gospel of Luke.

9

The Climax of
the Story

Author! Author!

In 333 B.C. Jerusalem is sacked, and upon Alexander's sudden death at the age of thirty-two, the Greek empire fractures and comes under the rule of one of Alexander's generals. In 198 B.C. Palestine, including Jerusalem, eventually comes under the rule of the Seleucids, a ruthless dynasty that attempts to control the Jews by humiliation and harsh reprisal for any infraction. In 169 B.C. the worst of the Seleucid rulers, Antiochus IV Epiphanes, begins a period of extensive persecution, slaughtering Jews in Jerusalem, defiling the temple and establishing Greek cult worship within the temple walls! This leads to the "Maccabean Revolt," which results in nearly 103 years of fairly independent self-rule, the reconsecration of the Temple and the re-establishment of Jewish culture. This period of relative freedom ends when General Pompey conquers Jerusalem in 63 B.C. and establishes Roman rule.

With the memory of freedom still fresh, the longing for the Son of David, the promised Messiah who will bring lasting peace to Israel, is intense. This is the historical, social and political backdrop of the New Testament. No wonder so many tired yet hopeful Jews had a hard time identifying with a rabbi, who spoke of loving one's enemies, as the Messiah they longed for. But the story of Scripture is God's story about setting all things right and it continues to be full of surprises and full of grace and truth.

GROUP DISCUSSION. On a piece of paper, complete this sentence: The most surprising person I ever met was _____. Include a brief explanation for your answer. Go around the group and have each person read their own summary.

PERSONAL REFLECTION. Recall a few surprising people and situations in your life, people who were different than you expected and events that unfolded in unexpected ways. How did you respond to them at the time?

The four Gospels in the New Testament give us a four-dimensional view and a quadraphonic rendition of the same story: the story of the incarnation of God's Son in the person of Jesus, the Christ. Three of the Gospels (Matthew, Mark and Luke) are termed "synoptic," as they see Jesus with the "same eye" and sing in the same key, though they have distinct voices, original audiences and intentions. All the Gospels are essentially eyewitness accounts of the person, teaching and activity of Jesus. However, John is the last disciple to write his Gospel and 90 percent of John's Gospel relates new stories to a new audience, those who have never heard or seen Jesus in the flesh (John 20:31). John's Gospel doesn't start with the Christmas story like Matthew and Luke do, or with Jesus' public ministry as in Mark. John's Gospel begins where the story of Scripture begins, "In the beginning" (Genesis 1:1). *Read John 1:1-18.*

---

1. Look back at the very beginning of the creation account in Genesis 1:1-3 in the light of John 1:1-5. What are the parallels in and comparisons between the two passages?

2. John 1:6-8 and 1:15 are an interlude focusing on John the Baptist. What does John, the Gospel writer, make clear in the summary?

Why would this be especially important for his first readers?

---

3. John 1:9-13 continues the introduction of the Word of God. What tensions do you see in these verses?

---

4. The impact of John 1:14 should be startling! It is significant that the words translated "made his dwelling" (NIV) or "lived among us" (NRSV) can also be translated "tabernacled" or "pitched a tent among us" in the original language. What does this indicate about the kind of relationship God established through the incarnation of the Word of God?

---

5. Not until John 1:16-18 is the earthly name of the Word revealed as God the Son. What characteristics of the Son are emphasized in this passage?

---

6. If you had never heard of Jesus before what would you find surprising, challenging and intriguing about this introduction to John's Gospel?

We move now to the evening before Jesus' arrest and crucifixion, which he spent with his disciples. After a meal, Jesus took an extensive amount of time teaching his disciples. Part of this conversation relates directly to the opening of John's Gospel. *Read John 14:8-14.*

7. How does Jesus explicitly clarify his relationship to God the Father in this passage?

8. In John 14:10-12 Jesus relates what he says (his words) to what he does (his works). How does Jesus use this to encourage these disciples to believe in him?

How do both the words of Jesus and the works of Jesus influence your faith as a Christian?

9. In John 14:13-14 Jesus talks about the importance of prayer in the life of faith (see also 16:23-28) and especially during times where faith is difficult and things seem hopeless. How is prayer both harder and more necessary during these times?

10. What are some things you can do to help you pray "in Jesus' name," to pray what Jesus would pray?

11. The focus of the Gospels is on who Jesus is, what he taught and what he did as God in the flesh to inaugurate the coming of God's kingdom and secure the way of salvation for God's people. How has your life been changed and shaped by your faith in Jesus as the eternal Word of the Father, God the Son?

Spend time expressing prayers of adoration using words that express ways you know the story of Scripture identifies Jesus (Emmanuel, True Vine, King, and so on), and end with a time of thanksgiving for your salvation through Jesus the Son.

Now or Later

Read through one of the Gospels in one sitting, pretending that you have never heard the story of Jesus. Before you begin, pray that God will help you be surprised like those who first encountered Jesus.

Between the Times: The four Gospels make it very clear that even Jesus' closest followers did not understand the real implications of his paradoxical kingship and kingdom. Dying to live, losing to gain, triumph through weakness, and a kingdom not of this world were not at all a part of the messianic expectation of God's people in first-century Israel. Jesus' death did not feel like a "Good Friday" for his followers. Saturday was the longest day of their lives. "Were we wrong?" had to be the question that haunted them. Even after the resurrection, it was hard to understand and believe what had happened (Mark 16:8; John 21:1-3). Even worship was doubtful for some (Matthew 28:17). Luke's Gospel overlaps the beginning of his second volume, the book of Acts, as it focuses on the ascension of Jesus as the prelude to the sending of the Holy Spirit on the church. Only with the coming of the Spirit will all the pieces fall together and begin to make sense to Jesus' disciples. Read Luke 24:13-53.

10

The Story Continues
New Cast, Global Tour

Acts 1:3-11; 11:1-30

Monday morning quarterbacks are the annoying evidence of the wisdom of hindsight. Saying "if I had known then what I know now" isn't just for middle-aged people looking back on the foolishness or naiveté of youth. "Connecting the dots" is actually a mark of a maturing faith. The coming of the Holy Spirit makes all the difference in how we understand Jesus, the kingdom of God and our world today.

GROUP DISCUSSION. Make a comprehensive list of all the mission agencies that members of the group have been involved in, financially supported or appreciated in some way. Talk about how the work of the Holy Spirit continues to this day in the church through the demonstration and proclamation of the gospel throughout the world.

PERSONAL REFLECTION: Recall the ways that you have been involved in the mission of the church through your local congregation or through parachurch agencies at home and abroad. What short-term or long-term mission opportunities are of particular interest to you?

The book of Acts begins by overlapping the ending of Luke's Gospel.

Since Luke is the author of both books, reading the ending of Luke and the beginning of Acts underscores the reality that the story of Scripture is one story. After the four Gospels, the New Testament is focused on the person and work of the Holy Spirit in the body of Christ, the church. The book of Acts records the first thirty years of the Spirit's work, from the period shortly after the bodily resurrection of Jesus in about A.D. 33 to the imprisonment of Paul in around A.D. 64. The first decade of the church comprises the first eleven chapters of Acts; the events of Acts 12 can be fairly precisely dated between A.D. 42-44. The last twenty years recorded in Acts focus on the expansion of the church through the missionary activity of Paul.

Near the end of the Upper Room Discourse, Jesus tells the disciples, "I tell you the truth: It is for your good that I am going away. Unless I go away, the Counselor will not come to you; but if I go, I will send him to you" (John 16:7). The ascension of Jesus and the sending of the Holy Spirit are inextricably connected. *Read Acts 1:1-11.*

---

1. What do you notice about the aspects of Jesus' life that are highlighted in Luke 1:1-5?

---

2. Acts 1:12 indicates that Jesus and the disciples were on Mount Olivet, just outside of Jerusalem. What is the central concern of the disciples forty days after the resurrection (1:6)? Why do you think this is?

---

3. Note Jesus' reply (1:7-8). What is the primary purpose for the empowerment of the Holy Spirit for the disciples?

4. A good eyewitness testifies to what they have clearly seen. How has the Holy Spirit given you insight concerning other people, the world and your own life?

---

5. Summarize how the ascension of Jesus is described in the passage and the importance of the ascension for Jesus' continuing work of salvation (1:9-11).

Fifty days after the Jewish Passover (not counting sabbath days), Jews gather in Jerusalem for an early harvest celebration, Pentecost. Acts 2 relates how the Holy Spirit comes on twelve disciples and about 125 Jews who were Jesus' followers. Then God calls his disciples to bring the gospel to the Gentiles. It takes three visions, several explicit and detailed commands, and an angelic visit to get Peter to preach the gospel to those who are the most despised by Jews. In the middle of Peter's nervous explanation of Jesus, the Holy Spirit is suddenly poured out on those gathered in the home of a Roman centurion! The news gets to Jerusalem before Peter returns, and the Jewish Christians are alarmed. *What is happening?* Peter recounts this surprising event. *Read Acts 11:1-18.*

---

6. The inclusion of non-Jews (the Gentiles) in the story of Scripture was intended from the beginning and was included in God's promise to Abraham (see study 3; Genesis 12:3). How does Peter argue his point in this passage?

7. How can Peter's argument help you witness to Christ Jesus amid the complex racial prejudices that mark the world today?

In the midst of increasing persecution, a Jewish-Gentile community of faith begins in the city of Antioch. The church continues its struggle to understand a community made of people so unlike each other! *Read Acts 11:19-30.*

8. Note where the Jewish Christians were from, where they went and who they witnessed to in verses 11:19-21. What is the outcome of this missionary effort?

9. In Acts 11:22-30 the church leaders in Jerusalem send Barnabas to assess the validity of the first Jewish-Gentile community. Why might Barnabas send for Paul (once Saul of Tarsus and a persecutor of the church) to help with the work?

Given his background, why is Paul an exceptionally suitable person for such a challenging ministry?

10. How might a charitable contribution from the potentially controversial church in Antioch help the church in Judea and Jerusalem trust God's work in this ethnically mixed Jewish and Gentile congregation?

11. As the story begun in Scripture continues in your life and in your faith community, what have been the biggest surprises in how God has worked?

12. Identify a challenge for the churches in your community that needs to be addressed in the light of the gospel of Jesus Christ, which calls us to both proclaim and demonstrate the love, justice and coming fullness of the kingdom of God.

Take time to pray for what God would have you do as a Spirit-empowered witness.

Now or Later

Recall a time when you have experienced some sort of racial prejudice and write out an account of the situation and your response and feelings at the time. How does the gospel of Christ's reconciliation make a difference in how you reflect on the experience?

Between the Times: Read Galatians and Philippians.

11

The Story Continues

The Final Curtain Opens

> ### *Hebrews 4:14-16;*
> ### *9:11-15, 10:19-25*

The work of Christ Jesus did not end with his ascension. Paul affirms that God "raised him from the dead and seated him at his right hand in the heavenly realms" (Ephesians 1:20). From this position of exaltation, Jesus, still fully God and fully human, is the mediator, the go-between, for the Christian and the church. Christians' identity and hope are secure in Christ. This is our assurance that the story of Scripture is, in fact, our story. In Christ, we are written into the story of God's promises.

GROUP DISCUSSION. Take out all the different forms of identification you have with you (driver's licenses, membership cards, and so on), and see who has the most cards or the least, the best picture or the worst, the oddest card or the most interesting. How are ID cards helpful and important?

PERSONAL REFLECTION. "Identity theft" is a serious crime that makes the victims of that kind of personal misrepresentation and financial violation feel threatened and vulnerable. Having an advocate who vouches for your identity and shields you from fraudulent charges or wrongful transactions is essential. Prayerfully reflect on the dynamics of "identity theft" and how your identity is securely kept in Christ Jesus.

Hebrews is written to Jewish Christians who are struggling to remain faithful to Jesus as they are squeezed harder between two opponents. One source of opposition is the persecution of Jewish communities by the Roman Empire, which greatly increased just before the destruction of Jerusalem in A.D. 70. The other source of opposition is the unbelieving Jews, those who did not believe that Jesus was the Messiah. Those who participate in Jewish-Christian fellowship and worship are ostracized from families, social groups and the work that they have enjoyed and loved all their lives. These Jewish Christians need to know that, in Christ, they have someone who understands who they are and encourages their steadfast faith. *Read Hebrews 4:14-16.*

1. Jesus is identified as the ultimate "high priest" in these passages. What does *Jesus* do as a high priest on behalf of God's people?

What does the mediation of Jesus enable the *believer* to do?

2. How does the mediation of Jesus to God for us and to us on God's behalf encourage honesty in our relationship with God?

3. Hebrews 4:15 underscores Jesus' identification with our sinfulness, as well as his sinlessness. How does this make confession of sin both harder and easier?

4. *Read Hebrews 9:11-15.* How does the identification of Jesus as sinless open up the way for believers to enter a new place and a new relationship with God (4:14, 16; 9:14)?

5. Because Jesus leads the way, the Christian has access to God's mercy and help (4:16). How have you experienced this mediating work of Jesus in your life?

6. How do the three persons of the Trinity—Father, Son and Holy Spirit—help you grow in holiness and Christlikeness?

7. How does the growth of holiness and the practice of worship shape your identity (and the identity of your faith community) as a Christian?

8. *Read Hebrews 10:19-25.* How does this passage summarize a believer's new identity and the life gained for us by Jesus through the way he has gone before us (10:19-22)?

9. How does Hebrews 10:23-25 picture the new identity of Christians in a community?

10. How has this study in Hebrews informed and encouraged your understanding of following Jesus in every facet of your life as a person whose identity is secure in Christ?

11. What can you do to help your prayers, personal devotional times and corporate worship better reflect the reality of Christ's ongoing work as our High Priest?

Spend times in prayers of praise to God for Jesus as our great and sinless high priest.

Now or Later

Find classic or contemporary hymns that celebrate the priestly work of Christ Jesus. The hymn "Jesus, Lead the Way" from the 1700s, "In Christ Alone" by Stuart Townend or William Dix's hymn (especially the last stanza) "Alleluia, Sing to Jesus" are good examples.

Between the Times: Read 1 John.

12

The Never-Ending Story

It's a Cast Party!

1 Corinthians 15:51-58;
Revelation 21:22—22:5

So, how does the story of Scripture end? At a new beginning. The New Testament gives us very few ideas about the last and unending chapter of God's story. The end of time and space as we know it, the judgment of the world, the final sanctification of the church as the bride of Christ, and the fulfillment of the kingdom in the new heaven and the new earth are all a part of the final chapter. But details are few and the sequence of events is far from clear. God has breathed into Scripture what he wants us to know, but he doesn't give the whole ending away! It is good to trust what is promised, but not entirely clear, to the wisdom of God.

GROUP DISCUSSION. Take a sheet of paper and complete this sentence in a lighthearted way: My perfect picture of eternal life is _____. Fold up the papers, and have each person pick one and guess who wrote each description. For instance, I've often kidded people that my idea of heaven is a comfy hammock in a huge library with access to all the authors who I might have questions for, *and* a good cook to bring me what I feel like eating (everyone knows there are no calories in heaven and everyone is the perfect size!).

PERSONAL REFLECTION. Take some time think about how your funeral might reflect your participation in the story of Scripture. What would you like to have said about you? What music would you like sung or played? What Scriptures would you have read?

In the first part of this study, we will see how Paul describes the bodily resurrection of believers on the day of the Lord. Earlier in the chapter, Paul affirms and describes the bodily resurrection of Christ and this is the basis for Paul's explanation of a long-standing mystery, "How are the dead raised? With what kind of body will they come?" (1 Corinthians 15:35). *Read 1 Corinthians 15:51-58.*

1. Point out several ways that Paul describes the resurrection of the body in this passage.

How have you heard the resurrection of the body addressed in funerals or memorial services for people of faith? What has been helpful or confusing at these times?

2. Paul quotes two passages from the Old Testament to celebrate the reality of the resurrection in 15:54-55. How does this declaration acknowledge the reality of suffering in life as well as celebrate God's triumph?

3. How does Paul want God's people to act in response to this exciting and triumphant promise of eternal transformation (15:58)?

4. What thoughts and feelings do you have as you read this passage?

The last chapters of the last book in the New Testament continue God's story as John describes a vision of the new heaven and new earth. Part of this vision is a depiction of the church, the bride of Christ, as a "Holy City, the new Jerusalem, coming down out of heaven and from God, prepared as a bride beautifully dressed for her husband" (Revelation 21:2). John continues his description of the bridal city and the return of God's people to the paradise of God's kingdom. *Read Revelation 21:22—22:5.*

5. Contrast Revelation 21:22-27 with the first three chapters of Genesis (refer also to studies 1 and 2 in this guide). What images of creation are altered, eliminated or transformed in these passages?

6. Note the restoration of Eden by comparing Revelation 22 to Genesis 2:1-14. How does the restoration pictured in Revelation surpass even the goodness and lavish abundance of Eden?

7. Revelation 22:2 notes the presence of the tree of life in the garden of the new Jerusalem. Contrast this idea with Genesis 3:24 when the access to the tree of life was ended. What does the reintroduction of the tree of life indicate in this passage?

8. Note the promises revealed in Revelation 22:3-5. How do these ideas help you think about the experience of eternal life in the kingdom of God?

9. End the study by thinking through what you have learned about the unity and focus from beginning to end of the story of Scripture. How will your continued study of God's Word be enhanced by understanding the big picture when you are focusing on a snapshot?

Read Revelation 22:16-20 as a prayer to end this study.

Now or Later

Identify someone in your life who needs the encouragement of God's story, and tell them what you've learned.

Leader's Notes

MY GRACE IS SUFFICIENT FOR YOU. (2 COR 12:9)

Leading a Bible discussion can be an enjoyable and rewarding experience. But it can also be *scary*—especially if you've never done it before. If this is your feeling, you're in good company. When God asked Moses to lead the Israelites out of Egypt, he replied, "O Lord, please send someone else to do it!" (Ex 4:13). It was the same with Solomon, Jeremiah and Timothy, but God helped these people in spite of their weaknesses, and he will help you as well.

You don't need to be an expert on the Bible or a trained teacher to lead a Bible discussion. The idea behind these inductive studies is that the leader guides group members to discover for themselves what the Bible has to say. This method of learning will allow group members to remember much more of what is said than a lecture would.

These studies are designed to be led easily. As a matter of fact, the flow of questions through the passage from observation to interpretation to application is so natural that you may feel that the studies lead themselves. This study guide is also flexible. You can use it with a variety of groups—student, professional, neighborhood or church groups. Each study takes forty-five to sixty minutes in a group setting.

There are some important facts to know about group dynamics and encouraging discussion. The suggestions listed below should enable you to effectively and enjoyably fulfill your role as leader.

Preparing for the Study

1. Ask God to help you understand and apply the passage in your own life. Unless this happens, you will not be prepared to lead others. Pray too for the various members of the group. Ask God to open your hearts to the message of his Word and motivate you to action.

2. Read the introduction to the entire guide to get an overview of the entire book and the issues which will be explored.

3. As you begin each study, read and reread the assigned Bible passage to familiarize yourself with it.

4. This study guide is based on the New International Version of the Bible. It will help you and the group if you use this translation as the basis for your study and discussion.

5. Carefully work through each question in the study. Spend time in meditation and reflection as you consider how to respond.

6. Write your thoughts and responses in the space provided in the study guide. This will help you to express your understanding of the passage clearly.

7. It might help to have a Bible dictionary handy. Use it to look up any unfamiliar words, names or places.

8. Consider how you can apply the Scripture to your life. Remember that the group will follow your lead in responding to the studies. They will not go any deeper than you do.

9. Once you have finished your own study of the passage, familiarize yourself with the leader's notes for the study you are leading. These are designed to help you in several ways. First, they tell you the purpose the study guide author had in mind when writing the study. Take time to think through how the study questions work together to accomplish that purpose. Second, the notes provide you with additional background information or suggestions on group dynamics for various questions. This information can be useful when people have difficulty understanding or answering a question. Third, the leader's notes can alert you to potential problems you may encounter during the study.

10. If you wish to remind yourself of anything mentioned in the leader's notes, make a note to yourself below that question in the study.

Leading the Study

1. Begin the study on time. Open with prayer, asking God to help the group to understand and apply the passage.

2. Be sure that everyone in your group has a study guide. Encourage the group to prepare beforehand for each discussion by reading the introduction to the guide and by working through the questions in the study.

3. At the beginning of your first time together, explain that these studies are meant to be discussions, not lectures. Encourage the members of the group to participate. However, do not put pressure on those who may be hesitant to speak during the first few sessions. You may want to suggest the following guidelines to your group.

☐ Stick to the topic being discussed.

☐ Your responses should be based on the verses which are the focus of the discussion and not on outside authorities such as commentaries or speakers.

☐ These studies focus on a particular passage of Scripture. Only rarely should you refer to other portions of the Bible. This allows for everyone to participate in in-depth study on equal ground.

☐ Anything said in the group is considered confidential and will not be discussed outside the group unless specific permission is given to do so.

☐ We will listen attentively to each other and provide time for each person present to talk.

☐ We will pray for each other.

4. Have a group member read the introduction at the beginning of the discussion.

5. Every session begins with a group discussion question. The question or activity is meant to be used before the passage is read. The question introduces the theme of the study and encourages group members to begin to open up. Encourage as many members as possible to participate, and be ready to get the discussion going with your own response.

This section is designed to reveal where our thoughts or feelings need to be transformed by Scripture. That is why it is especially important not to read the passage before the discussion question is asked. The passage will tend to color the honest reactions people would otherwise give because they are, of course, supposed to think the way the Bible does.

You may want to supplement the group discussion question with an icebreaker to help people to get comfortable.

You also might want to use the personal reflection question with your group. Either allow a time of silence for people to respond individually or discuss it together.

6. Have a group member (or members if the passage is long) read aloud the passage to be studied. Then give people several minutes to read the passage again silently so that they can take it all in.

7. Question 1 will generally be an overview question designed to briefly survey the passage. Encourage the group to look at the whole passage, but try to avoid getting sidetracked by questions or issues that will be addressed later in the study.

8. As you ask the questions, keep in mind that they are designed to be used just as they are written. You may simply read them aloud. Or you may prefer to express them in your own words.

There may be times when it is appropriate to deviate from the study guide. For example, a question may have already been answered. If so, move on to the next question. Or someone may raise an important question not covered in the guide. Take time to discuss it, but try to keep the group from going off on tangents.

9. Avoid answering your own questions. If necessary, repeat or rephrase

them until they are clearly understood. Or point out something you read in the leader's notes to clarify the context or meaning. An eager group quickly becomes passive and silent if they think the leader will do most of the talking.

10. Don't be afraid of silence. People may need time to think about the question before formulating their answers.

11. Don't be content with just one answer. Ask, "What do the rest of you think?" or "Anything else?" until several people have given answers to the question.

12. Acknowledge all contributions. Try to be affirming whenever possible. Never reject an answer. If it is clearly off-base, ask, "Which verse led you to that conclusion?" or again, "What do the rest of you think?"

13. Don't expect every answer to be addressed to you, even though this will probably happen at first. As group members become more at ease, they will begin to truly interact with each other. This is one sign of healthy discussion.

14. Don't be afraid of controversy. It can be very stimulating. If you don't resolve an issue completely, don't be frustrated. Move on and keep it in mind for later. A subsequent study may solve the problem.

15. Periodically summarize what the group has said about the passage. This helps to draw together the various ideas mentioned and gives continuity to the study. But don't preach.

16. At the end of the Bible discussion you may want to allow group members a time of quiet to work on an idea under "Now or Later." Then discuss what you experienced. Or you may want to encourage group members to work on these ideas between meetings. Give an opportunity during the session for people to talk about what they are learning.

17. Conclude your time together with conversational prayer, adapting the prayer suggestion at the end of the study to your group. Ask for God's help in following through on the commitments you've made.

18. End on time.

Components of Small Groups

A healthy small group should do more than study the Bible. There are four components to consider as you structure your time together.

Nurture. Small groups help us to grow in our knowledge and love of God. Bible study is the key to making this happen and is the foundation of your small group.

Community. Small groups are a great place to develop deep friendships with other Christians. Allow time for informal interaction before and after each study. Plan activities and games that will help you get to know each other. Spend time having fun together going on a picnic or cooking dinner together.

Worship and prayer. Your study will be enhanced by spending time praising God together in prayer or song. Pray for each other's needs and keep track of how God is answering prayer in your group. Ask God to help you to apply what you are learning in your study.

Outreach. Reaching out to others can be a practical way of applying what you are learning, and it will keep your group from becoming self-focused. Host a series of evangelistic discussions for your friends or neighbors. Clean up the yard of an elderly friend. Serve at a soup kitchen together, or spend a day working on a Habitat house.

Study 1. The Beginning of the Story: Characters, Setting, Plot. Genesis 1—2.

Purpose: To discern God's character through his creation of all that is out of nothing, and to take note of God's ordering of creation, including the intention for human relationships with God and with others both in caring for creation and in family relationships.

General note. It is always helpful to remember that holy Scripture is a Jewish story, inspired (God-breathed, 2 Tim 3:16) by God and written through faithful Jews.

Group discussion. Be sure to have a set of small sheets of paper that look the same. If necessary, let the group know that this preliminary exercise is important to acknowledge the attitudes and presuppositions that we can often bring to the opening chapters of Genesis. These opinions need to be expressed in order to set them aside so that you can focus on what the text says in a fresh way. Many people assume one of two things about these opening chapters, things that keep them from appreciating God's purposes for why the story of Scripture starts the way it does. First, it is not uncommon to think that the first chapters of Genesis are like a cartoon or a simplistic caricature of something too difficult to understand. So these chapters are often skimmed over or skipped—as if they're not all that important in the long run. Second, it may be even more common to reduce these chapters to the scientific explanation for creation. This can result in arguments about the age of the Earth, issues of evolutionary theory and the like.

The opening chapters of Scripture are intended neither to be a simplistic cartoon nor a scientific explanation. You might want to bring Zero candy bars (or some other symbol for *nothing*) to the study as a fun reminder that this is the number in Genesis that matters most. It's a good way to make the point that the God who created all that is out of nothing (*ex nihilo*) could do so as fast or as slowly as God desired. The age of the earth is not the point of

Genesis 1. Who God is as the Creator is the point. "Did Adam have a navel?" is not the point of Genesis 2. God's loving relationship with human beings is the point.

Personal reflection. These ideas are designed for individuals who desire a new look at some old texts that are often troublesome and unsettling in a variety of ways. The Scripture story is meant to be understood for its own purposes, and it is good to set aside ideas that have been imposed on texts that they are not meant to address. God's Word is utterly reliable and tells the truth God wants us to know. It may not answer all our questions, but God's Word can often call into question our assumptions about faith and life.

Question 1. This is an observation question intended for the group to notice the overall sequence of God's order in creation and the variety of ways the Creator brought all creation about as the Spirit of God was "hovering" and the creative Word of God was spoken. The hints in this opening passage of God's story pointing to the Trinity are just that, hints, and should not be a focus of what is observed in the passage.

Question 2. The use of several verbs in Genesis 1 indicates how creative God was in creating! For instance, God separated one thing from another (light from darkness, v. 4). God "made," "gathered" and "let" some things fulfill their intended designs. God "set" certain things and "created" anew at particular junctures.

Question 3. It is important to note the rhythmic sequence of the creation of the cosmos and its summation from "evening to morning." A new day is signaled as the period of light ends so that the rhythm of life begins with rest as darkness falls. The seventh day is a measure of God's full rest as he "ceases" (the Hebrew word *sabbath*) from his creative work. Throughout the story of Scripture, God's people are invited into God's rest in order to know him intimately (e.g., 1 Kings 8:56; Ps 37:7; Heb 4:9-10) and experience the peace of God's grace.

Question 4. This question is focused on the verses that are the basis of the Jewish and Christian affirmation that creation is good and not evil. The declaration of creation as good also indicates a moral dimension within time and space that is imposed on creation by God himself. This is why there is a sense of right and wrong, good and bad, embedded within the universe itself, and not determined by human beings but by the Creator from the very beginning. Both creation care and our attention to biblical ethics are manifestations of how God's people see the world (summarized as the Judeo-Christian worldview).

Questions 5-6. Like a signpost, an image of something points to the ultimate destination, the original idea or the real person. "The governing work of God was seen to be accomplished by people. . . . The image provides the capacity not only to serve in the place of God (his representative containing his essence) but also to be and act like him" (John H. Walton, Victor H. Matthews and Mark W. Chavalas, *IVP Bible Background Commentary: Old Testament* [Downers Grove, Ill.: IVP Academic, 2000], p. 29).

Question 7. God's work of creation was orderly and purposeful, not haphazard or random. God brought light out of darkness and order out of chaos in a sequence of events that culminates in the creation and blessing of man and woman. The cosmos was created to provide for and sustain life, as well as function to benefit people who bear the Creator's image. Humanity was intended to reflect God's benevolent dominion over creation. The image of God is reflected in the benevolent ordering of social and familial relationships between men and women. All that we do should contribute to bringing order out of chaos, light out of darkness.

Question 9. It is important to affirm that the man, at this point in the story, really had the freedom to obey or disobey God's command. The capacity for human free will is embedded in this story—as is God's sovereignty, his capacity as the only One who fully knows, sees and understands what lends itself to good or evil. When anticipating the Fall and the disobedience of the woman and the man in the next chapter, it is helpful to remember the argument in the New Testament that Jesus, seen as the "second Adam," was perfectly obedient in every way (Rom 5:19; 1 Cor 15:22, 45; Phil 2:8; Heb 5:8). Jesus, fully human as God incarnate, was equally free to obey or disobey (see Heb 4:15). This is one significant way to understand that the story of Scripture is one story from beginning to end!

Question 11. "Man" (NIV) or "humankind" (NRSV) are good translations of the Hebrew word *adam,* which is used in Genesis 1:26-27; male and female together are *adam.* In Genesis 2, in the particularizing account of human creation, the male is identified as *ish* (of the clay) and the woman is called *ishshah,* the feminine form of *ish.* The name Eve for the woman is introduced as part of the aftermath of events in Genesis 3. Using the language and words as they are used in the Scripture can be very helpful in understanding what the story actually says and means.

Question 12. The woman was created for the man as a fully suitable partner for him in the work humanity was intended to do together and for the families they were to establish together. The Hebrew word for "helper" in Genesis 1:18 is *ezer* and does not connote hierarchy, inferiority or subordination. *Ezer* is often associated with God as our helper in the Old Testament.

Someone might bring up the title of a well-known book, *Men Are from Mars, Women Are from Venus.* This title focuses on our differences instead of highlighting our shared humanity, reflecting the disruption of the Fall, rather than God's intention for men and women from the beginning.

Study 2. The Story Continues: A Twist in the Storyline. Genesis 3.
Purpose: To understand the ramifications of sin and appreciate God's faithfulness to eventually restore creation and redeem his people.
Group discussion. It may be necessary to clarify that this exercise needs to be kept on the lighthearted side of childhood memories. The idea is not to surface truly painful memories, experiences of great wrongdoing or issues of being victimized by sin as a child. See the note below. You can just make it a discussion if you think the drawing of names would be uncomfortable in your group.
Personal reflection. The intention of this recollection (including the lighthearted group exercise suggested) is not to trivialize humanity's sinful nature, but to help illustrate that people become aware very early in life of this deep flaw rooted in our *being,* not just reflected in our *behavior.* Children often don't know how to harden their hearts concerning sin as well as adults often do. It's good to recall when it was that God began to create in us a longing for the Good News through the recognition of the Bad News!
Question 1. Bible students and scholars have wondered about the presence of the tempter-serpent in the garden for as long as people have read this story. However, the focus of the biblical text "speaks not of evil invading, as though it had its own existence, but of creatures rebelling. His malevolent brilliance raises the question, which is not pursued, whether he is the tool of a more formidable rebel" (Derek Kidner, *Genesis,* The Tyndale Old Testament Commentaries [Downers Grove, Ill.: InterVarsity Press, 1967] p. 67). The important focus for our study is on how the tempter casts doubt on God's words. This is the foundational dynamic for temptation and sin throughout the Bible and is seen very clearly in the temptations Jesus faced (Mt 4:1-11; Lk 4:1-13).
Question 2. Temptation in this passage begins in the *ear,* the first inkling of doubt leads the *eye* to look at the tree, the *heart* then finds its fruit desirable, the *hand* then plucks what is off-limits, the *mouth* tastes what was forbidden, and the *mind* decides to invite a partner (who was right there and listening!) to join in the rebellion. This anatomy of sin is also clearly pictured in the story of David's sin with Bathsheba in 2 Samuel 11:2-4. If there is time, read this short passage as part of the discussion.
Question 3. The idea isn't to pull deep, dark secrets out of people. Simple personal stories are helpful responses here, and general comments about public figures and the woes of front-page news can help discern the patterns of sinful behavior that betray the sin nature of everyone.
Question 4. You could have your group first describe, or even act out, the scene if you wish.

Note that it is the Lord God who comes looking for his rebellious image-bearers. The questions God asks are not asked due to a lack of knowledge or information on God's part, but they are asked to make the human couple account for and confess their own behavior. It's like a parent looking at a child with some forbidden chocolate smeared on face and shirt and asking, "What is that on your face and shirt?" The parent knows what it is but wants the child to own up to it!

Question 6. The lack of curse language focused on the man and woman is significant in the overall story of Scripture. Even here there is a subtle hint that God knew that he would have to deal with the curse of sin himself in the incarnation of the Son. Paul makes the point in the New Testament that the curse that was due the human family was taken on Jesus the Son in the crucifixion (Gal 3:13). It's a stunning parallel in the story of Scripture that the sinful disobedience of the first Adam (*ish* and *ishshah*) at this tree in the garden is undone by the obedience of the second Adam on the tree at Golgotha (Rom 5:18; 1 Cor 15:22).

Question 8. Partnerships that were intended to be perfect become compromised by difficulty and pain. The work for both the man and the woman was to be facilitated with ease and rewarded with fruitfulness, but it becomes toilsome and infested with things that don't belong. And the man and woman's relationship as perfectly fitting partners becomes one of hierarchy and subordination. Deceit, wrongly focused desire and yielding to temptation fractured human relationships. The consequences of sin deeply corrupted God's best gifts for those who bore God's image.

Question 10. Note that God kills an animal that he deemed good on the sixth day (Gen 1:24-25). For the first time, death is graphically seen and God begins to institute the sacrificial system that will be central in the story of redemption that is unveiled in the rest of Scripture (Ex 12; Lev 4; Heb 9:22). How God's heart must have broken for what had been lost! Think about how much worse it could be if living as sinful people in a fallen world was everlasting, unending. The removal of the tree of life not only introduces a limit on life expectancy but, with this, a limit on our time to continue sinning and suffering.

Study 3. The Story Is Our Story: Everyone Has a Part. Genesis 12:1-5; 15.
Purpose: To consider how God's plan for salvation continues through the human family. From *ish* and *ishshah* in the garden, through Noah's family in the flood, to Abraham's family (with whom God inaugurates the promise of salvation for the world), God faithfully continues to make things right.

Group discussion. Help group members to be as specific as possible. Depending on the group, you might have each person take a piece of paper and summarize in one sentence the hardest or most surprising move in their lives. Then put them in a basket and, drawing one at a time, try to guess who wrote each one. The idea is to help the group appreciate the faith it took for

Abraham and Sarah to move to a new place in order to know, worship and be faithful to God.

Personal reflection. This recollection is itself a practice of faithfulness. Many of the psalms were written as an exercise in looking back and discerning personal lessons learned and acknowledging the faithfulness of God. You may want to write a prayer or a new psalm that summarizes your insights and understanding.

Question 1. Most scholars are quite sure about the location of biblical Haran. It is the modern town of Harran, population 8,800, on the Turkish side of the Syrian border and near the Euphrates (M. W. Chavalas, "Haran," in *Dictionary of the Old Testament: Pentateuch,* ed. T. Desmond Alexander and David W. Baker [Downers Grove, Ill.: InterVarsity Press, 2003], p. 379). It is interesting to note that Haran was noted for its study of astrology and had a tower that was used for calculating distances and directions, as well as for stargazing and celestial navigation.

Question 3. Lot does become a significant hardship in Abraham's life (Gen 13:5-13; 14:11-16; and 19, one of the most horrific chapters in the Bible). Whether or not it was obedient for Abraham to take Lot has been debated by scholars for years, but the consequences of Lot's life and choices did cause pain and difficulty for the patriarch.

Question 5. Abraham and his wife, Sarah, were well past "middle-age" in that day and had suffered from some sort of infertility, because they remained childless. This fact makes the idea of Abraham's offspring inheriting the land a challenge to faith. On the other hand, Abraham's lack of options for a child with Sarah provided the patriarch an opportunity for a faith absolutely invested in the promise and person of God. Please see the note below under "Now or Later."

Question 6. The extravagance of God's promise makes faith radically necessary. Only the God who promises such a thing can bring about its fulfillment. This is God's pattern for faith throughout the story of Scripture. You might ask group members to suggest other episodes in Scripture that call for a radical faith in a similar way.

Question 7. It is important to note that Abraham's question in verse 8 is a question about *how* God will keep his promise, not a doubt about *if* God will keep his promise. This is very similar to Mary's question to the angel Gabriel (Lk 1:26-37) concerning the promised conception and birth of Jesus. Mary's question (Lk 1:34) concerns her virginity, not God's ability to accomplish what was promised. Note that the visible sign for Mary, instead of dust and stars, was the pregnancy of Elizabeth, her long barren relative (Lk 1:36-38).

Question 8. "The covenant ritual resembles that of Jeremiah 34:18. In its full form, probably both parties would pass between the dismembered animals to invoke a like fate on themselves should they break their pledge. Here,

however, Abram's part is only to set the scene and guard it from violation"
(Derek Kidner, *Genesis,* Tyndale Old Testament Commentaries [Downers
Grove, Ill.: InterVarsity Press, 1981], p. 124).

Question 9. The idea of this darkness as "terrifying" (NRSV) or "thick and
dreadful" (NIV) will be a recurring motif throughout the story of Scripture
when God makes and keeps promises to his people. From Sinai where God's
law was given, to Calvary where God's Son becomes the final sacrifice, the
fear of the Lord is marked by a darkness that overwhelms those to whom
God speaks. It is also important to note that Abraham is asleep when God's
presence, like a "smoking firepot," moves between the dismembered animals. Abraham is not an equal partner in this covenant ritual. This is God's
promise, and God alone will keep it.

Question 10. The suffering of Abraham's offspring heralds a history that
God anticipates and reveals to the patriarch. Also note that the detailed defi-
nition of the inheritance (vv. 18-21) underscores the concrete reality of what
God will do for Abraham and his offspring.

Now or Later. As a group leader, it will be important to be sensitive to any
person in the group that has a particularly painful hardship where faith
is difficult (infertility, battling cancer or other life-threatening illnesses).
The passage in Genesis is focused on God's continuing plan for ultimate
salvation, and you may have to redirect group members to focus on this big
picture. Some sorrows and sicknesses will only be overcome by God's grace
in the eternal realm where all tears are wiped away.

Study 4. The Story Continues: A World Premiere. Exodus 2:23—3:17.

Purpose: To see how God continues to keep his promises despite the reluc-
tance and lack of faith of his people.

Group discussion. Help the group members to think about a *specific* time,
place and challenge to act by giving time to think of a concrete example. Be
flexible about the amount of time given to this, but encourage members to
summarize and not add more details than are needed.

Personal reflection. This recollection is intended to help you think through
how God's persistent faithfulness has helped you in times when you were
reluctant to be faithful.

Question 1. Note the repetitive way *God* is used with a series of action verbs
in Exodus 2:24-25, as well as how completely God's plan is outlined for Moses in Exodus 3:7-12.

Question 2. The text just records that the people complained, cried for help
and groaned, but it is not clear that their efforts were directed toward God
as faithful prayer. They just needed someone to help get them out of the op-
pressive situation they were in, not necessarily out of Egypt altogether. Even
during the escape and long wandering journey back to Canaan, there were

many who wanted to go back to Egypt!

Question 4. God's identification as "the angel of the Lord" occurs approximately fifteen times in the Old Testament and always indicates an extraordinary manifestation of the Lord God to a specific person or in an unusual situation. "The coming of the Angel is the coming of Yahweh in all his sovereignty, yet Yahweh announces the coming of the Angel as though speaking of someone else. . . . We see in the account of the burning bush that it is by means of his Angel that . . . the Lord himself is present" (J. A. Motyer, *The Message of Exodus*, The Bible Speaks Today [Downers Grove, Ill.: InterVarsity Press, 2005], p. 51).

Question 5. Miraculous manifestations in the story of Scripture always point to some characteristic of God. God doesn't just heal, provide for and deliver people; God is the Healer, Provider and Deliverer. John's Gospel makes this very clear when Jesus declares himself to *be* what he *does* (I am the resurrection, I am the good shepherd, etc.). The angel of the Lord appears in a bush that is aflame but not consumed, demonstrating that, although truly present in created time and space, God is not limited to or overcome by what he has created. The bush really burned, so this was not a case of Moses' personal interior experience of "enlightenment" (seeing what others could not) but the bush was not burned up, showing that God was not the bush but the Creator of all created things. This God, who brought all that is out of nothing, could and would bring his people out of Egypt!

Question 6. Throughout the story of Scripture people are called by God to worship, and they are told how God desires to be worshiped. Even in the New Testament, it is God the Son who must make a way for us to "approach the throne of grace" (Heb 4:14-16). We should come "with confidence," but remember, at the same time, that it is a *throne* of grace, not an easy chair.

Question 7. God wants to involve Moses and his concern for his people, but God himself is the Deliverer, not Moses. You may want to refer the group to (or briefly summarize) the passage that directly precedes the text being discussed. Exodus 2:11-15 relates how Moses unsuccessfully executed his own plan for delivering his people and was rebuffed by fellow Israelites for his efforts. This is why Moses fled Egypt and became a sheepherder in Midian. This also accounts for part of Moses' skepticism that God had the right man for the job! Moses left Egypt as an outlaw.

Question 8. "The God of Abraham, Isaac and Jacob was a God of many titles and one single name. . . . Yahweh ('The Lord') would no longer be a mere form of address but would tell its own story about the divine nature and do so in a way immediately relevant, endlessly satisfying and bafflingly enigmatic" (Motyer, *Message of Exodus,* p. 69). This underscores the idea noted in question 5: God manifests his character (who he is) by keeping his promise to put all things right (what he does). The story of Scripture is God's story of what he has done, because of who he is, so that we might become who we really are as the beneficiaries of his grace—most especially in Christ Jesus by the Spirit.

Question 10. It might be helpful to use the movie *Dances with Wolves* to help group members think through and enjoy this exercise. The movie title indicates the name given to a pioneer Army soldier because of what they saw him *do.* A person might be one who "Always Wants More" today, but would like to grow into a person who is "Content with Life" tomorrow.

Study 5. Knowing the Story: Studying the Script. 2 Samuel 6.

Purpose: To see the importance of knowing the story through studying the Scripture in order to know, obey, love and worship the Lord in a way that pleases *him.*

Group discussion. You will need a large sheet of paper or white board to list each idea suggested by group members. Leave this up during the study, and check off or add items as the study progresses (or at the end of the study).

Personal reflection. All leaders have strengths as well as weaknesses, and this was true of David and his leadership. David was a man after God's own heart (1 Sam 13:14; Acts 13:22), but one of his strengths as a leader was a willingness to learn from his mistakes.

Question 1. Thirty thousand men of Israel had died at the hands of the Philistines when the Ark was captured in battle (1 Sam 4:10-11). You should familiarize yourself with this story as preparation for this study by reading 1 Samuel 4—7:1. Second Samuel 6 indicates that David may have taken 30,000 men with him as a show of might, and he may have done his homework concerning the Ark's capture and subsequent return to Israel.

Question 3. The death of Uzzah took David by surprise. The king felt like he was doing the right and noble thing out of his love for God and out of his desire to see the faithful worship of Yahweh as a central, unifying factor in Israel's life as a nation. David's spiritual leadership would rightly be questioned in this situation. He had not done his homework concerning God's instructions for transporting the Ark, nor how Yahweh had structured the worship of Israel for his own purposes and pleasure.

Question 4. Most congregational worship is designed as a manifestation of all of these things. The discussion at this time can't be exhaustive but should underscore the importance of knowing the story of Scripture and the instructions given to design worship that is pleasing to God.

Question 5. The observance of the law in the transport of the Ark of the Covenant (2 Sam 6:3, 13) and the contrast between the large numbers of instruments (2 Sam 6:5, 15) may indicate a much more careful approach to the celebration. Uzzah's demise was certainly on the minds of those Levites designated to carry the Ark. After only six anxious steps ("Oh! I hope we are doing this right!" might have been their silent prayer), they stop and celebrate their success (2 Sam 6:13).

Question 6. During the three months following Uzzah's death, David did the homework in Scripture that he should have done before. His joy was not dampened by his reverence, but it was now fettered to God's Word and made wise and right. The fear of the Lord isn't just the beginning of wisdom (Prov 1:7); it is a mark of biblical worship. David's attitude and question recorded in 2 Samuel 6:9 should have guided his preparation for worship from the very beginning.

Question 7. First Chronicles 13 is a retelling of 2 Samuel 6:1-11. First Chronicles 15:1-3 relates the successful entry of the Ark into Jerusalem and highlights the fact that David had prepared a place for the Ark by pitching a tent for it in the city, according to the instructions given to Moses. Sacred space, sacrifice and community blessing are pictured as important components of Israel's worship.

Question 8. The relationship of Saul and David was turbulent and complex for at least twenty-five years prior to Saul's death (1 Sam 17—31), and there was a power struggle between David and the house of Saul after his death (2 Sam 2—4). At one point, Saul, who had reluctantly given his daughter Michal to David in marriage (1 Sam 18:17-29), took her away and gave her to another man (1 Sam 25:44). Second Samuel 3:14-16 relates the sad story of David demanding the return of Michal after at least fifteen years of marriage to another man she had grown to love. You may want to point out that the final verse of this study indicates that David had no sexual relations with Michal for the rest of her life (2 Sam 6:23).

Question 9. Being more conscious of the Lord's presence than even the presence of others is helpful in keeping the pleasure of the Lord central to worship instead of our own preferences. Humility before the Lord helps us know and keep our place in worship. The congregation is not the audience to be pleased by worship leaders. The congregation is wholly centered on God who is the ultimate focus of and only audience for our worship.

Question 11. *Parenting in the Pew* (InterVarsity Press) is a book that helps both parents and children (toddlers through teens) engage in worship that is focused on pleasing God.

Study 6. Knowing the Story: A Remedy for Stage Fright. Isaiah 7:1-14.

Purpose: To consider the challenges to faith in times of fear and vulnerability, and the importance of knowing the story of God's promises and believing in God's unfailing power to keep the promises he makes.

Group discussion. Help the group focus on childhood situations that are no longer threatening or painful. The idea is to get some perspective on how help offered in times of strife is not always appreciated at the time. The wisdom of godly intervention is often only appreciated after the dust settles! If some group members focus on times of adult crisis, the real impact of how hard it is to believe and hope can be quite poignant.

Personal reflection. Wise counsel is often appreciated only after some time has passed between the turmoil and its resolution. Considering the help you've received to bring reconciliation in major or minor family disputes can often help teach you how to patiently help others in similar situations. A hopeful word spoken against all odds can be insensitive (even if offered with good intentions). However, a wisely spoken and true word can still be hard to hear without some sign of proof. If you've been in a situation like that, what "proof" was needed in order to believe?

Background note. There were only three kings that ever ruled the twelve tribes: Saul of Benjamin, David of Judah and David's son Solomon (1 Kings 1—11). During the reign of Solomon's son, Rehoboam, there is a civil war (1 Kings12—14) led by Jeroboam who was from the tribe of Ephraim. From this time on, two nations are established. Only Benjamin stays faithful to the Davidic throne in the south, becoming the nation of Judah. The more numerous but rebellious northern tribes reject the covenant promise God made with David (2 Samuel 7) that only the descendents of David will ever rule God's people, but they keep the majority of the land and keep the name of the patriarch, Israel. However, some prophets, like Isaiah, designate the Northern Kingdom by the tribal name Ephraim.

Question 1. Isaiah 7:1 is a great verse in which to observe the clear differentiation of the Northern Kingdom, Israel (called Ephraim by Isaiah), and the southern kingdom, Judah. This episode in the story of Scripture takes place in the mid-700s B.C., and the foreign nation Aram (also called Syria, a nation directly north of Israel's border) had joined forces with Israel in the westward expansion of mighty Assyria. (It's not vital for the focus of this study, but you can find summaries in 2 Chronicles 28:5-8; 17-18 of the two futile attempts made by Israel and a foreign ally to bring the dynasty of David to an end.)

Question 2. The issue at stake is faith in God's Word and his promises. Will the king and his people believe Yahweh's promise to David and his descendants (2 Sam 7), or attempt to defend themselves by forming their own ungodly alliance with another nation in an effort to save themselves? "The description here deliberately pinpoints the particular crisis of the day. Ahaz is the 'house of David' and what he now does will be decisive for the future of the dynasty. . . . The ten-year-old alliance [between Aram and Israel] would not as such constitute news or a cause of panic, but intelligence reports of large-scale troop movements in Israel . . . would and did. Another invasion was impending before which king and people panicked" (J. Alec Motyer, *The Prophecy of Isaiah* [Downers Grove, Ill.: InterVarsity Press, 1993], p. 81).

Question 4. Shear-Jashub's name is sign of God's unfailing faithfulness to his people, but at the same time, it is a reminder that only a minority, a remnant, of God's people will be faithful and know the salvation of God. The way has always been narrow and few are those who find it (Mt 7:13-14). The most vulnerable threat to a walled city is its water supply. During the reign of Ahaz, Jerusalem's water supply was above the ground and vulnerable. Isaiah is directed to meet Ahaz at a place where he will sense his greatest helplessness. Judah's next king, Hezekiah, improves the security of Jerusalem's water supply (Is 22:9-11), but at this time, a siege against the city would be disastrous.

Question 5. *"Be careful, keep calm/* 'watch yourself and be still' does not mean 'watch out for the enemy but do not worry' but rather . . . 'Be careful to do nothing' " (Motyer, *Prophecy of Isaiah,* p. 81). The clarity of the command intensifies the vulnerability that Ahaz must feel, but God can command this of him because God knows the vulnerability and weakness of Aram and Israel.

Question 6. Draw attention to the fact that the prophet does not call the kings of Judah's enemies by their names, but he belittles their status before Ahaz by calling them only "the son of." The situation that seems like such an ultimate threat to Ahaz and Judah will come to nothing! Help the group identify with this dynamic—how has faithful dependence on God delivered us from evil? Ultimately this leads us to the cross of Jesus Christ, but there are penultimate situations where not acting, not doing, not defending ourselves, but wholly trusting God to prevail, has proven the greatness of God.

Question 9. This is the only time God ever offers someone a blank check, an opportunity to determine a sign that will bolster a person's faith to believe an impossible thing. God certainly gives signs to others, but he announces the sign. Only here does God offer a person the opportunity to name it! God, who loves Ahaz and Judah, knows that putting all their faith in him and doing nothing will be extremely difficult. So Yahweh makes this extraordinary offer because he understands human weakness.

Question 10. Ahaz turns down God's extraordinary offer in a retort that sounds pious. In reality it was an expression of religious pride. To refuse such an offer proved that Ahaz was an unbelieving man and therefore could not act in faith. This will spell the end of Ahaz and his reign but not God's faithfulness to deliver his people and fulfill the prophecy concerning the enemies of Judah.

Question 11. The dynasty of David is continuing to unravel despite the occasional revival and faithful king in Judah. The refusal of Ahaz to believe is a reflection of Judah's increasing faithlessness and apostasy. This is why God gives the sign he does, a sign that David's only perfect descendant will forever sit on the throne and faithfully govern God's people.

Question 12. Two Hebrew words are involved with the idea of a "young woman" or a "virgin" in Isaiah 7:14. *Bethulah* means "virgin," and *almah* means simply an unmarried female. *Almah* is the word used in this text and refers both to Isaiah's wife who was a virgin only until she married (see Is 8:1-4) and, typical of much Old Testament prophecy, also anticipates a final fulfillment in the person and life of Jesus. Mary's virginity was intact as Jesus was conceived by the Holy Spirit (Lk 1:26-38). In Ahaz's "impossible" situation, God promises a sign that will once and for all prove that "nothing is impossible with God" (Lk 1:37).

Study 7. The Story Continues: Taking It on the Road. Daniel 1.

Purpose: To understand the distinction between being faithful and being effective by learning how to be both without compromising what matters while under the authority of others. In telling the story of Scripture, it is important that our lives bear character marks as those who have been shaped by the story.

Group discussion. In order to appreciate the challenges faced by Daniel and his friends, it's helpful to recall some of what it takes to live in a new society in which the customs, culture and language are different from one's own. Be sure you have identical papers and a container for the drawing.

Personal reflection. What we learn in awkward or foreign situations (and how we learn it!) helps us know how to be helpful to the newcomer or foreigner who visits or begins to live in the place we call home.

Background. The Jews who survive the conquest and remain in the land intermarry with the Assyrians and further compromise the worship of Yahweh by idolatry (2 Kings 17). These descendants of Israel become known as "Samaritans" in the story of Scripture, and they are increasingly despised by their southern cousins in the nation of Judah.

Question 1. *Israelites* (Dan 1:3) refers to the captives from Judah and Jerusalem. Since the Northern Kingdom (Israel) had ceased to exist well over a hundred years earlier, other nations, and eventually Judah herself, will designate Jews by using the patriarchal name. It's interesting to note that learning "the literature and language" of the foreign land was key to the formation of the new inhabitants of the empire. Chaldea is the Assyrian name for the region of southern Babylon, and in the Old Testament, Chaldea is used interchangeably with Babylon. Knowing the story of the new culture was vital to becoming Babylonian; just as knowing the story of Yahweh and his people was vital to remaining faithful to their One God. Being called by new Babylonian names was a key attempt to change the identity of the captives.

Question 2. Nebuchadnezzar II reigned as the emperor of Babylon from 605-562 B.C. The conquest of the former Canaanite territories happened in stages of political and military strategy. From exacting tributes from vassal states to the final destruction of major cities and strongholds within conquered territories to minimize resistance, Babylon established its empire. However, Nebuchadnezzar failed to invade Egypt in 601, and Judah's king Jehoiakim renounced the vassal status of Judah and "sought the support of Egypt in his rebellion. This disloyalty eventually proved fatal and led to the first Babylonian siege of Jerusalem in 597" (*IVP Bible Background Commentary: OT,* p. 729). The final destruction of the city occurred eleven years later. Daniel 1:2 makes it clear that "the exile is not due to the inability of Judah's God to defend Jerusalem, but rather is brought about by a deliberate act of her God" (Ernest Lucas, *Daniel,* Apollos Old Testament Commentary [Downers Grove, Ill.: IVP Academic, 2002], p. 52).

Question 3. It is important to note that Daniel made up his mind (he "resolved") before he asked the "palace master" (NRSV) or "chief official" (NIV) for permission to refuse the royal rations.

Question 4. Bible scholars have offered a variety of suggestions for why Daniel may have considered the king's food "defiling" (e.g., the food's possible association with pagan temple worship or the lack of kosher preparation of the food in the kitchens of the court). The first example is not clear from the text, and the latter example would not explain Daniel's refusal of the king's wine as well. The emphasis in Scripture is the idea that the refusal centered on the idea that it was the *king's* food (Dan 1:5, 8). Daniel 11:25-26 mentions the idea that "plots against the king by those who have eaten such 'royal rations' are unexpected and particularly reprehensible. To accept and eat such food was, apparently, to commit oneself to loyal allegiance to the king" (Lucas, *Daniel,* p. 54). The protest of these four young Jewish men may have been one way to express their loyalty to Yahweh as the only one worthy of their full allegiance.

Question 6. The concern of the official for keeping his job and his head is not just focused on the physical appearance of Jewish men but also the attitude they might display. The official is open to Daniel's suggestion if they can cooperate and do well in other ways. Daniel and his friends must not show outward defiance or make their protest with observable dissent.

Question 7. Note that Daniel did not argue with the chief official, but he suggested a trial under the watchful eye and cooperation of the guard, a junior official. The length of time, ten days, "is short enough not to arouse suspicion of outright defiance, but long enough for the effects to show" (Lucas, *Daniel,* p. 55). Daniel 10:3 indicates that, later on, when Daniel had his own table as a Babylonian official, meat and wine were a part of his diet. The point of the passage is not the issue of vegetarianism or the prohibition of alcohol but of Daniel's resolve to keep his ultimate allegiance to Yahweh with integrity.

Question 9. It may be helpful after some initial comments to direct the group to some other biblical passages that picture God's people as citizens of

God's kingdom who need to live faithfully and productively in a world that is not our home. Jeremiah, a prophet who lived through the siege of Jerusalem, admonished the captives how to live in a foreign land. Read Jeremiah 29:4-7, as well as Romans 12:2; Philippians 3:20; and 1 Peter 2:9-12.

Question 10. Much of the book of Daniel is a continuation of the story of how Daniel and his friends resisted assimilation, partially withdrew at times for particular reasons, and continued to live in, work for and witness within a place that was not their home. It is stunning to recognize that 600 years after their witness, "Magi from the east came to Jerusalem and asked 'Where is the one who has been born king of the Jews? We saw his star in the east and have come to worship him'" (Mt 2:1-2). Daniel and his friends knew the story, lived the story and told it well.

Study 8. The Story Continues: After the Theater Burns Down. Haggai 1—2:19.

Purpose: To better recognize the Lord's priorities, as well as his patience in times of hopelessness (when there is just too much to do, and we feel like it all won't be good enough even if we get it all done), and to better appreciate the need for holiness—not just as a religious *end* but as the necessary *means* along the way of life with all its challenges and demands.

Group discussion. If you are aware of group members who have dealt with the aftermath of a flood, fire, tornado or other disaster that was devastating to a whole family or community, ask them before the study if they would like to describe what they went through to recover. What made it hard? What helped? It is good to ask ahead, because significant disasters, even years later, can still be emotionally challenging to share with others. If the group has mostly experienced disasters vicariously, just help guide the discussion to uncover how members have experienced "compassion fatigue."

Personal reflection. Most people have needed help to function well and wisely in an overwhelming season of life. It's good to recall the resources and people who helped you make it.

General note. Haggai is a great book to study with colored pens or markers. You may want to print out this short book and supply colored pens or markers for group members to use in underlining repeated expressions, parallel ideas, time markers in the text, promises, commands and so on. (Group members can also do this in their bound Bibles if they like the idea.) Note how the timetable is noted in Haggai (1:1, 15; 2:1, 10, 18, 20). This helps underscore the sense of revival and energy that God stirred up in the people through the ministry of Haggai.

Question 1. Darius seized the Persian throne in September 522 B.C. The date first noted in Haggai is (by our calendar) August 29, 520 B.C.

The reiteration of prophetic language is very apparent in Haggai, occurring seven times in the opening eleven verses. This language is important to note whenever reading the prophets, and its absence by false prophets is always significant.

Question 2. The mention of "paneled" houses is a significant indicator that the people had secured adequate shelter for some time and had invested in rather elaborate remodeling and decoration. Paneled houses were often associated with homes built for royalty, rulers and the upper class. Paneled houses hadn't led to a sense of security or satisfaction, but were simply a product of the desire for more and better. The point is not that the rebuilding of the temple should have commenced before people had roofs over their heads, but the point is that rebuilding the place of sacrificial worship had been delayed and neglected to the point of forgetfulness.

Question 4. Through Haggai, the Lord directed the people to take the first step: gathering some supplies needed to rebuild the temple. When an overwhelmingly huge task looms ahead, just getting started by lining up what you need to get the job done helps! "Baby steps" of faith matter when God presents us with a big challenge.

Question 5. Drought, as with all natural disasters, subjects people to real helplessness. Situations of total vulnerability can be used by God to redirect faithless people to recognize their need for repentance and a renewed attentiveness to the Lord and his will for their lives.

Question 6. It is important to note how often the Scripture in Haggai carefully records how everyone needed to consider, repent and engage in the work. Over and over again, the text explicitly addresses Zerubbabel—the governor (the Jews could have a governor but not a king)—as the political leader from the tribe of Judah, a vassal state paying taxes and cooperating with Persian authorities—Joshua (a Levite and high priest, who was the religious leader) and all those who were the remnant of God's people. Those who feared the Lord were careful to listen, believe and obey. These families, who had weathered an exile due to rebellion and disobedience, had learned something of the consequences that come from not having the wisdom that comes from rightly fearing the Lord. The date given in Haggai 2:1 is October 17, 520 B.C., only seven weeks after the first prophecy.

Question 7. The work began, and the people began to reminisce about "the good ole days" and the lavish beauty of Solomon's temple. It would be natural for the old timers, who had seen Solomon's temple, to tell Haggai's generation about its splendor and to grieve again over all that had been lost. Timber for repairs had been gathered from the surrounding area, but what about the gold and silver? Mourning for the devastation was an understandable part of the restoration process, and the Lord knew the people needed encouragement to see things from his perspective. The glory that filled Solomon's temple would pale in comparison to this second temple. God knew that in *this* temple, whose restoration would continue through the reign of Herod the Great, his Son would teach as a twelve-year-old, overturn the tables of corruption, dispute with those who refused to see him as the promised Messiah, and raise his voice as the Living Water and Light of the world! This was splendor only God could see. In God's promise was the hope the people needed to continue their work.

Question 9. Haggai's questions point to the fact that holiness must be intentional. Holiness can't be passed on from one person to the next or one generation to the next. Consecrated meat (Hag 2:12) will still be holy in the folds of the priest's garment, but it cannot make holy the things that touch the garment. That which is unholy does defile all that it touches (Hag 2:13). Only God, not the work of the people, can render a place or a people holy.

Question 10. The repetition of the date in 2:10 and 18 indicates how significant the date was for the Lord to honor and the people to remember. Haggai reminded Judah of God's faithfulness before any rebuilding began (Hag 2:16) and during times of hardship and poverty (Hag 2:16-17). The date was December 18, 520 B.C. In the darkest time of the year, God promised his blessing to these people who had returned to worship Yahweh and continued to believe God's story.

Study 9. The Climax of the Story: Author! Author! John 1:1-18; 14:8-14.

Purpose: To consider the story in its original context of the incarnation of God in Jesus Christ in order to better appreciate God's extravagant grace in salvation.

Group discussion. It is hard to overestimate how different Jesus was from the Messiah Israel expected. This exercise is designed to help the group appreciate, through their own experiences, how often our expectations get in the way of seeing how things really are.

Personal reflection. Some people handle surprises better than others! How we handle unexpected things in our lives can sometimes indicate how we might respond to the surprising events of faith, including those in Scripture.

Question 1. "John's opening echoes Genesis 1:1, but whereas Genesis refers to God's activity at the beginning of creation, here we learn of a being who existed before creation took place. . . . So we actually start before the beginning, outside of time and space in eternity. If we want to understand who Jesus is, John says, we must begin with the relationship shared between the Father and the Son" (Rodney Whitacre, *John*, IVP New Testament Commentary [Downers Grove, Ill.: InterVarsity Press, 1999], p. 50).

Question 2. In several places in his Gospel, John goes out of his way to clarify who John the Baptist was and who he wasn't. In the late first century there seems to have been a few rather sectarian groups who focused on ideas or people at the expense of keeping Jesus central to the faith. John's Gospel, because it was written after nearly all the eyewitnesses to Jesus' life were dead, clarifies ideas and dispels a few rumors that seem to have had some influence in the early Christian community.

Question 3. John 1:12-13 maintains the dynamic tension between human free will and God's sovereignty that is apparent throughout Scripture. "Why do some believe and others do not? . . . If we only had verse 12, the answer would be human response . . . the imagery of coming alive as God's children suggests the focus here is on the power that produces divine life . . . exercised by the person. . . . On the other hand, if we had only verse 13 the answer would be divine initiative" (Whitacre, *John*, p. 55). The mystery and grace of salvation is pictured paradoxically in Scripture. If one emphasizes one part of the tension at the expense of the other, you end up with less than the mystery that makes this God's story and not ours!

Question 4. Jesus exemplified the glory of God by being full of both grace and truth. This, too, is how we can mature as those who give God glory through our lives. The fullness of both grace and truth was only perfectly manifest in Jesus, but it is good for us to develop this balance. We are usually more full of one than the other. If people are more full of truth, they can tell you what's wrong or right, but they fail to communicate God's grace. If they are only full of grace, they can be unclear or silent about the truth. Both fail to be love and light in ways that reflect the gospel of Jesus.

Question 5. "Verse 17 is sometimes read as a rejection of Moses and the law. But the relation here between Jesus Christ . . . and Moses and the law is one of fulfillment—the graciousness of God revealed in Scripture has now been perfectly manifested in Jesus. . . . If the glory of the divine presence that filled the tabernacle (and later the temple) has now come to us in Jesus, then he is the place where we now seek God's presence" (Whitacre, *John*, pp. 60-61).

Question 7. The Upper Room Discourse in John's Gospel properly begins in John 13:31 after Judas, the betrayer, leaves the supper to instigate the arrest of Jesus. This extended teaching ends after Jesus' prayer in chapter 17. The whole of John's Gospel focuses on who Jesus is as the eternal Son of the Father, but this is a particular emphasis of the Upper Room Discourse.

Question 8. John's Gospel makes it very clear that Jesus is what he does, and that he does because of who he is. In John 6 Jesus declares himself to be the "bread of life" after he feeds thousands of people with a small lunch. In John 8—9 Jesus identifies himself as the "light of the world" and then heals a man who was blind from birth. In John 11, just before raising Lazarus from the dead, Jesus tells Martha, "I am the resurrection and the life." It is notable that Jesus does not say "I do" this or that but "I am"; in so doing he identifies himself with the divine name of Yahweh revealed to Moses in

Exodus 3. This identification was very clear to those who heard Jesus make this claim. They called it blasphemy and tried to stone him! (See Jn 8:58-59 for another example.)

Question 10. Knowing God's will through God's word is essential to praying "what Jesus would pray." It's often helpful to pray the words of Scripture itself to learn and practice this. It might be helpful to direct the group to consider one of the psalms or one of Paul's prayers in the New Testament as good places to start. It may also be helpful to pray with an elder in the faith who can help guide your prayer and help you mature as a disciple.

Study 10. The Story Continues: New Cast, Global Tour. Acts 1:3-11; 11:1-30.

Purpose: To underscore the importance of the ascension of Jesus, who is the eternal embodied reality of and promise for human redemption. Also, to understand how the glorification of the Son is manifest in the presence of the Holy Spirit in the body of Christ.

Group discussion. Prepare a good-sized writing area (a white board, a tablet on an easel or paper taped to a wall) that everyone can see well for the listing of mission agencies. These should include foreign and domestic, both denominational and parachurch. The comprehensive list will be surprisingly long for most groups and will be a good visual reminder throughout the study that the mission of the church is expansive and dynamic. God is still at work in a variety of ways through his people by the Spirit.

Personal reflection. It is important to note that the Holy Spirit moves distinctly in each believer and in each community of faith for God's own purposes. What area of the world, what sort of work, what particular things interest you in the ongoing work of God?

Question 1. Both Luke's Gospel and Acts were addressed to Theophilus, a name that means "friend of God." It is not clear if Theophilus was a person who sponsored Luke's research or a literary device used to address all people who would be friends of God. However, the use of the honorific title ("most excellent") for Theophilus in Luke 1:3 seems to indicate that Theophilus was a person who asked Luke to investigate the story of Jesus and the early spread of the Christian church.

Question 2. As Jews of the first century, the disciples continued to reflect their longing for the Son of David to deal with the oppressors of Israel and reestablish the kingdom of God as a political and religious reality for God's people. Not until the Holy Spirit was poured out on the disciples did they gain the insight needed to understand what Jesus meant when he told them in a variety of ways that his kingdom was not of this world (Lk 17:20-21; Jn 18:36). Acts 1:12 mentions that Olivet was a "Sabbath day's walk" from Jerusalem, within the distance allowed by Jewish law to walk on the Sabbath, about three-quarters of a mile.

Question 3. In the incarnation, Jesus humbled himself (Phil 2:5-8) for the sake of our salvation and could willingly curtail his divine knowledge. Matthew 24:36 and Mark 13:32 are parallels to this incident in Acts 1:7. The book of Acts follows the geographical outline reflected in Acts 1:8. The church, by its empowered witness, grew outwardly from Jerusalem to surrounding Judea into Samaria and out to the world in all directions.

Question 5. The ascension of Jesus occurred forty days after Easter (Acts 1:3). Ascension Day falls during the sixth week after Easter on a Thursday, and it may be, arguably, the least celebrated day in the whole church calendar for a liturgical year. Yet without the ascension, our salvation, like the story of Scripture, would be incomplete. Without the ascension, the resurrection of Jesus would have been limited to an event like that of Lazarus, a short-term victory over death, which was a long-term enemy. But the story of Scripture records the ascension as the continuation of the resurrection triumph of Jesus. The incarnation of God the Son continues eternally because Jesus was raised and ascended bodily so that redemption includes all that makes us truly human. Christ remains united to our humanity so that we may, through the person of the Holy Spirit, be united to him. The New Testament makes it clear that Jesus Christ, the Son of God, was incarnate, suffered, died, rose, ascended and "will come back in the same way" (Acts 1:11). If group members are familiar with historical church creeds, like the Apostles' Creed or the Nicene Creed, it may be helpful to refer to the inclusion of the ascension in the ancient creeds of the church as an indication of how the early church recognized the importance of the ascension in the redemptive work of Christ Jesus.

Question 6. It is hard to overestimate the impact the prejudice between Jews (including Jewish Christians) and non-Jews makes on the New Testament. Racial reconciliation is a central concern in Paul's conversion (Acts 9) and his subsequent ministry and writing. Racial reconciliation is the biggest challenge that the early church faced. Much of the persecution that Rome brought against the Jews and the church is due to the unrest caused by the dispute over Gentile inclusion in the church of the New Testament. Reading the New Testament in the light of this problem is very helpful in understanding the story of Scripture.

Question 8. Acts 6:8—8:1 relates the death of the first Christian, a non-Palestinian Jew named Stephen who was a deacon in the church. Note in Acts 11:20 that the Jews who preached the gospel to Gentiles in Antioch were also not from Palestine. Jews who lived outside the boundaries of ancient Israel were those who continued the witness to Gentiles that had begun with Peter.

Question 9. Acts 9:1-31 relates the miraculous conversion of a powerful Jewish leader, Saul of Tarsus, who had been committed to a violent and murderous rampage against the church. Saul, transformed as the apostle Paul, recounted his story in Galatians 1:11-24. These texts clearly reflect how hesitant the early church was to trust the conversion of Saul. Barnabas needed help with the work, and who better to help than someone who had once been a part of the problem?

Study 11. The Story Continues: The Final Curtain Opens. Hebrews 4:14-16; 9:11-15; 10:19-25.

Purpose: To see the ongoing mediation and work of Christ after his ascension in the continuing story of Scripture.

Group discussion. Talk about the importance of ID cards in everyday life (like helping with transactions, allowing certain functions and verifying membership in a group). This exercise is intended to highlight how important identity is to people. If anyone has been the victim of identity theft in the past, have them share how it felt and what steps were taken to correct the situation. The passages in this study focus on our identity as secure in Christ and on Christ's role in "getting us into places," the work of salvation and our membership in the body of Christ.

Personal reflection. If you or anyone you know has been the victim of identity theft in the past, you are aware of how threatening and disrupting this crime can be. It takes a lot of help to straighten out the mess of identity theft.

Question 1. The high priest had a particular part to play in the temple sacrificial system. Once a year the high priest alone would act as a go-between, a mediator, to offer a sacrifice for the sins of the people and go behind the innermost curtain in the temple where the Ark of the Covenant was kept. Prior to offering a sacrifice for the people, the high priest had to offer a sacrifice for his own sin. The contrast here is with the sinless Jesus, the ultimate high priest. This contrast was even more notable because the priesthood in the first century was widely known to be corrupt.

Question 2. Christians should readily recognize and own up to sinful behavior. The temptations of life don't take God by surprise, because Jesus has "been there and *not* done that!" Jesus knows what tempts us in our humanity, and he offers to help us in those times to escape temptation (1 Cor 10:13). The church should be the last place where we hide our sin because it is not hidden from God. In Christ, we find a new identity as God's repentant and forgiven people.

Question 3. There is in Christ Jesus a two-way movement of mediation. Nothing in the Christian life is unmediated by the Son. Prayer, worship, confession, repentance, forgiveness and relationships with others are all part of our relationship with God and God's relationship with us who are in union with Christ.

Question 4. It is wise to recognize that mercy and help are found at the *throne* of grace. The boldness of the Christian is only possible because Jesus, the high priest, has gone before us and made a way. Mercy, help and grace are always and forever unmerited and undeserved. Christians follow Jesus boldly but also with careful dependence on his unique and sinless worthiness.

Question 5. Note how the ascension of Jesus is both visible and physical, and it is tied to the promise of his return "in the same way." When Jesus goes before us into the holy of holies, he serves as our mediator in the full presence of God. Christ, our perfect, fully human mediator, mediates for us in every way and in every aspect of our humanity—for our spiritual, emotional, mental and physical life . . . everything!

Question 6. Sanctification is the process of being made holy by the indwelling presence of the Holy Spirit. Day-by-day growth in understanding, desiring and manifesting God's righteousness and love is accomplished by the Spirit. See Philippians 1:6.

Question 7. The practice of daily prayer, Bible reading and study, and other spiritual disciplines are used by God to strengthen right living in our lives. The biblical and historical patterns of worship provide Christians with an opportunity to rehearse the story of God's redemption in Christ Jesus. The living God calls us to worship, and we enter with praise and confess our sinfulness to hear words of forgiveness and reconciliation, to submit to God's Word, to confess our faith, to feast on grace, and to offer gifts committing ourselves to the ongoing mission of God in the world. Through this pattern and practice of worship, God's people catch God's rhythm for all of life.

Question 9. The Day in verse 25 refers to the day of Christ's return. Although eagerly awaited for a long time, every day brings the return of the ascended Lord closer. For persecuted Christians, like the readers for whom Hebrews was written, the longing for a new beginning can feel intense.

Question 11. Taking more care in how we address God in prayer or conduct ourselves in worship can help us remember the necessity of depending on Jesus as our go-between. Reverence and freedom are marks of relying on the mediation of Christ.

Study 12. The Never-Ending Story: It's a Cast Party! 1 Corinthians 15:51-58; Revelation 21:22—22:5.

Purpose: To better understand the resurrection of the dead and the final consummation of the kingdom and reign of God in the new heaven and new earth.

Group discussion. Have identical pieces of paper or 3 x 5 cards and writing instruments for this exercise. This discussion starter is intended to help group members identify thoughts and feelings, hopes and longings concerning eternal life. These ideas are often not biblical and a bit of a caricature, but they can still give us a sense of how we think about ultimate rest and fulfillment.

Personal reflection. Thinking about the end of one's earthly life can be an exercise of hope as well as an encouragement to remain faithful until the end.

General note. Two important ideas about heaven are very clear in Scripture. First, eternal life is embodied. As Jesus was raised and ascended bodily, believers, too, will be raised bodily and share in the transformed and eternal life of Christ Jesus. In fact, the resurrection of the body is the very thing that brings final redemption to all creation (Rom 8:19-23). Second, the kingdom of God is the establishment of God's unrivaled reign in the new heaven and new earth where righteousness is at home (2 Pet 3:13) and the wholeness of God's perfect peace *(shalom)* has done away with all the effects of humanity's sinful rebellion.

Question 1. " 'Sleep' was a common euphemism for death. . . . Old Testament prophets often employed the image of the trumpet which was used to assemble people for convocation or war; here, as in a daily Jewish prayer of the period, it refers to the final gathering of God's people at the end" (Craig Keener, *IVP Background Commentary: New Testament* [Downers Grove, Ill.: IVP Academic, 1993], p. 488).

Paul is aware that some believers will be living on the day that Christ returns, but they too will undergo the same transformation as will the believers who have died. Be confident that the God who created the entire cosmos by his spoken word and out of nothing can certainly raise those who have returned to dust.

Question 2. Paul quotes Hosea 13:14 and part of Isaiah 25:6-10. You may want the group to read the Isaiah passage as it is also a part of the text in Revelation that we'll read in the second part of this study.

Question 3. Help the group notice the striking contrast between the triumphant crescendo of God's final victory on our behalf and the need for believers to just continue living life, day in and day out, in steady faithfulness to the work of the Lord. If this were music, the double-forte loudness beginning at the end of 1 Corinthians 15:54 suddenly changes to the quiet pianissimo of the disciple's life of labor. In our lives, much of what we do might seem unimportant, disappointing or pointless. But Scripture assures us that even the most mundane and ordinary work for God is not done in vain but is meaningful to God.

Question 5. The contrast of day and night in both Genesis and Revelation is quite stunning here. After the Fall the idea of night, particularly in the New Testament, is often used to reflect on a time for "deeds of darkness, sin and evil" not just a designation of time (Jn 11:10; Eph 5:8; 1 Pet 2:9). This distinction and contrast would have been understood by John's first readers. In the kingdom of God there is no "night" in this sense, and there will be no deeds of darkness.

Question 6. The passage bears remarkable similarity to Isaiah's prophecy. One can compare Revelation 21:23-26 with Isaiah 60:3, 11 and 19, or Revelation 21:27 with Isaiah 52:1. The point is to help the group sense the connection of John's vision in Revelation with the story of Scripture. Revelation is too often read as a weird, esoteric puzzle that is disconnected from the rest of Scripture. However, John's vision is a revelation of mystery, not a concealment of history. John's vision was first intended to spur the church to faithfulness for its mission to the world in the light of the church's promised victory in Christ. Revelation should be read for this same purpose today.

Question 8. The imagery used indicates the return of life without death or suffering; eternal life is restored to God's people.

Question 9. You may want to recall the lighthearted descriptions of heaven that you began the study with. What about those longings will be fulfilled in the *shalom* of God's kingdom?

Prayer. If you are studying with a group, read these verses in unison.

TIMELINE FOR BIBLICAL HISTORY (approximate dating)

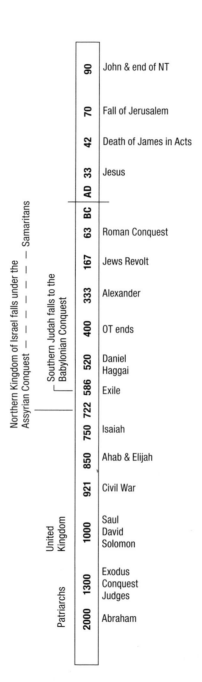

	Patriarchs	United Kingdom							Northern Kingdom of Israel falls under the Assyrian Conquest – – – – – – Samaritans				Southern Judah falls to the Babylonian Conquest					AD				
2000	1300	1000	921	850	750	722	586	520	400	333	167	63	BC	33	42	70	90					

Abraham — 2000
Exodus / Conquest / Judges — 1300
Saul / David / Solomon — 1000
Civil War — 921
Ahab & Elijah — 850
Isaiah — 750
Exile — 586
Daniel / Haggai — 520
OT ends — 400
Alexander — 333
Jews Revolt — 167
Roman Conquest — 63
Jesus — AD 33
Death of James in Acts — 42
Fall of Jerusalem — 70
John & end of NT — 90

KINGS AND PROPHETS IN THE OLD TESTAMENT

UNITED KINGDOM
Saul 1050
David 1000
Solomon 960

JUDAH		921 Civil War	ISRAEL	
Rehoboam	922-915		Jeroboam I	922-901
			Nadab	901-900
Abijah	915-913		Baasha	900-877
Asa	913-873			
			Elah	877-876
			Zimri	seven days
Jehoshaphat	873-849			
			Omri	876-869
			Ahab	869-850
Jehoram	849-842		Ahaziah	850-849
Ahaziah	several months		Joram	849-842
Athaliah	842-836		Jehu	842-814
Joash	836-797			
			Joahaz	814-798
			Jehoash	798-782
Amaziah	797-769		Jeroboam II	783-748
		Amos		
Uzziah	769-734		Zechariah	6 months
			Shallum	1 month
		Hosea	Menahem	748-738
Jotham	734		Pekahiah	738-736
Ahaz	734-715	Isaiah	Pekah	736-732/1
			Hoshea	732/1-723/2
Hezekiah	715-687	Micah		

Northern Kingdom, Israel,
falls to the Assyrians 722 B.C.

Manasseh	687-642		
Amon	642-640		
Josiah	640-608	Zephaniah Jeremiah	
Jehoahaz	3 months		
Jehoiakim	609-597	Nahum	
Jehoiachin	3 months	Habakkuk Ezekiel	
Zedekiah	597-587		

Southern Kingdom, Judah,
falls to Babylonians 586 B.C.

Daniel

Post-exile: Haggai, Zechariah, Malachi

This chart shows the kings of the United Kingdom, which divides in 921 B.C. after the civil war between Rehoboam and Jeroboam. Judah, the kingdom in the south, is on the left, and Israel, the Northern Kingdom, is on the right. The spacing indicates how the kings of each kingdom coincided, and the Old Testament prophets (in the middle) are placed near the kings they ministered to.

What Should We Study Next?

A good place to continue your study of Scripture would be with a book study. Many groups begin with a Gospel such as *Mark* (20 studies by Jim Hoover) or *John* (26 studies by Douglas Connelly). These guides are divided into two parts so that if twenty or twenty-six weeks seems like too much to do at once, the group can feel free to do half and take a break with another topic. Later you might want to come back to it. You might prefer to try a shorter letter. *Philippians* (9 studies by Donald Baker), *Ephesians* (11 studies by Andrew T. and Phyllis J. Le Peau) and *1 & 2 Timothy and Titus* (11 studies by Pete Sommer) are good options. If you want to vary your reading with an Old Testament book, consider *Ecclesiastes* (12 studies by Bill and Teresa Syrios) for a challenging and exciting study.

There are a number of interesting topical LifeBuilder studies as well. Here are some options for filling three or four quarters of a year:

Basic Discipleship
Christian Beliefs, 12 studies by Stephen D. Eyre
Christian Character, 12 studies by Andrea Sterk & Peter Scazzero
Christian Disciplines, 12 studies by Andrea Sterk & Peter Scazzero
Evangelism, 12 studies by Rebecca Pippert & Ruth Siemens

Building Community
Fruit of the Spirit, 9 studies by Hazel Offner
Spiritual Gifts, 8 studies by R. Paul Stevens
Christian Community, 10 studies by Rob Suggs

Character Studies
David, 12 studies by Jack Kuhatschek
New Testament Characters, 10 studies by Carolyn Nystrom
Old Testament Characters, 12 studies by Peter Scazzero
Women of the Old Testament, 12 studies by Gladys Hunt

The Trinity
Meeting God, 12 studies by J. I. Packer
Meeting Jesus, 13 studies by Leighton Ford
Meeting the Spirit, 10 studies by Douglas Connelly